BRITAIN'S EUROPEAN HERITAGE

BRITAIN'S EUROPEAN HERITAGE

L L O Y D   A N D   J E N N I F E R   L A I N G

with drawings by Priscilla Wild

ALAN SUTTON PUBLISHING LIMITED

First published in the United Kingdom in 1995
Alan Sutton Publishing Limited
Phoenix Mill · Far Thrupp · Stroud · Gloucestershire

British Library Cataloguing in Publication Data

Laing, Lloyd
Britain's European Heritage
I. Title II. Laing, Jennifer
941

ISBN 0-7509-0463-1

Library of Congress Cataloging-in-Publication Data applied for

Typeset in 10/15½ New Baskerville.
Typesetting and origination by
Alan Sutton Publishing Limited.
Printed by
Hartnolls, Bodmin, Cornwall.

Contents

List of Plates

List of Figures

Figures drawn by Priscilla Wild, except Figs 13 and 14.

List of Maps

Prologue

Britain has been physically separated from the Continent for eight thousand years – a mere moment in the Earth's timespan, and a very short period in the story of man's time upon it. It is not surprising therefore that the islands have tended to mirror developments on the Continental land mass, and to be subject to the changes of fortune of their Continental neighbours. These influences have fluctuated in intensity. Partly because the British Isles have not, for most of that time, been unified, influence from the rest of Europe has been unevenly distributed, some areas traditionally enjoying links denied to others.

Introductions from Europe have varied from languages, town and village sites, rabbits, roses and grapes, to gardens, romantic love, Christianity, crossbows, hats, and diseases. Contributing countries include France, Switzerland, Germany, Scandinavia, Italy, Spain, Portugal, Greece, and the Low Countries. Some have made major contributions to modern society, others more subtly pervaded British life, still others apparently had little lasting effect.

The extreme south of Britain was naturally subject to settlement from, and trade with, the Continent: for example there were links between Brittany and Dorset in the pre-Roman Iron Age and between Kent and northern Gaul. Subsequently the south was especially influenced by Rome and later the Anglo-Saxons. To this day French is widely spoken in the Channel Islands.

Scotland and north-eastern England were more open to influences from northern Europe – there were Norse settlements in the early Middle Ages and links between north-east Scotland and Germany in the Late Bronze Age, and between Scotland and France in the Middle Ages.

Western Britain, the 'Irish Sea Zone', was open to influences which came from southern Europe and the Mediterranean. In the later fifth and sixth centuries AD pottery from the east Mediterranean and Christianity from southern Gaul travelled northwards through the Irish Sea, just as pottery and wine from Bordeaux did in the twelfth and thirteenth centuries. The Irish, too, have strongly influenced the coastal areas of Wales and Scotland, to the point of bequeathing the name Scotland (after the Scots of Ireland).

These broad divisions are capable of greater refinement, when consideration is given to seaways, riverways, and the disposition not only of surviving barriers such as mountains but now-vanished features such as forests. Such differences have contributed to the creation of modern regional identities.

Political unity within the British Isles has had a chequered history. In later prehistoric times, and by inference, earlier, the entire area was tribal with, as far as can be ascertained, constant changes of regional alliances. The Romans conquered Wales and England south of Hadrian's Wall; the Anglo-Saxons after them eventually created England itself. It was under the Normans that influence extended to Scotland, and Ireland was politically under British rule from 1171 until 1921. Northern Ireland has remained British to the present. The position of Ireland as part of the British Isles has therefore fluctuated, but for the purposes of this book its relationship to the area under scrutiny changes according to the period. Sometimes it is counted as Britain, at others as part of the 'rest of Europe'.

Since the Union with Scotland in 1707 in particular, an increasing emphasis has been placed on Britain's uniqueness and individuality, presumably in order to foster unity between the different elements. There is no doubt that a discernibly 'British' culture and outlook has been developed in the past but, as this book will argue, the European character of the islands has never been lost, and at many times substantial portions of Britain have been economically, intellectually, politically, and emotionally very much part of the European scene. The close modern economic links are merely following precedents laid down for hundreds of thousands of years.

From the 1972 Treaty of Rome onwards, Britain's economic fortunes have been increasingly linked to those of the rest of Europe, to the point where there is currently considerable debate over where sovereignty lies. Certainly much legislation applicable to Britain is now created abroad – a situation that has never existed on such a scale except during the Roman period.

This state of affairs is perhaps not as innovatory as it might appear to people brought up in the twentieth century, who have been instilled with pre-1945 concepts of Britain's isolation. Although the time since 1707 represents eleven generations, it is a mere 0.06 per cent of the time since the arrival of the first hominids, when Britain and the Continent were literally one and the same landmass. As will be seen, despite the massive social upheavals of the past thirty years in particular, the population of the islands has remained remarkably static for many centuries, and underlying trends are not easily uprooted. The European past manifests itself today in language, landscape, communications routes, placenames, architecture, the legal system, the class system and the system of land tenure.

Perhaps the most surprising evidence for immigration in the past has come as a result of medical research, which has built up a genetic map of the British Isles. This distinguishes, for example, the 'Celtic' areas from those of their 'Anglo-Saxon' neighbours, and the population of the Shetlands shows strong connections with Scandinavia, reflecting the intensive Norse settlement. In the central Lake District, the genetic pool is distinctive from that found in the periphery of the region and displays links with areas from which the Norse came.

The Danes have left their strongest genetic legacy in north-east Derbyshire, where there is also a high density of placenames of Danish origin. In East Anglia there is a marked genetic divide between the populations of Norfolk and Suffolk, which coincides with the modern county boundary. This may echo differences in the genetic background of the North and South Angles who came from the Continent.

The population of Cornwall and Devon shows genetic differences from the rest of England, and displays features in common with people in South Wales and Brittany.

One other useful clue to the impact of immigrant cultures in Britain is provided by a study of placenames, although these do not always reflect the extent of control of a population. Most notable in this connection are Roman placenames which have survived only in very rare instances. A few placenames seem on linguistic evidence to belong to a pre-Celtic past and relate to natural features – the names for the Rivers Wey and Wye (which have the same root) are a case in point.

The main substratum of placenames in Britain as a whole is, however, Celtic and mostly relates to natural features, such as rivers, although words for hills, and less frequently woods and headlands, also occur.

By far the greatest number of placenames in England are either Anglo-Saxon or Scandinavian in origin, reflecting the importance of first the Anglo-Saxon and then the Viking settlements.

The Norman influence on placenames was not as extensive as might be expected – some were simply transferred directly from France and some were changed by French scribes having difficulty with the old English form, for example.

Some placenames reflect other immigrants in medieval England, such as Flimby ('village of the Flemings') in Cumbria, or Wiggonby in the same county, which comes from Wigan, a Breton French name.

Although the presence of these and other incomers is well attested, the ways in which they became assimilated into the British population have been much contested in the past two decades. In the nineteenth and early twentieth centuries it was fashionable for archaeologists, inculcated with views of colonialism and empire-building, to see the early history of Britain as the story of successive 'waves' of invaders who introduced 'superior' cultural trends from the Continent. Whenever the archaeological record showed a sudden change in lifestyle – pottery, habitations, weapons, technological skills, and so on – it was easy to assume that these were the result of, probably hostile, incomers.

In the aftermath of the Second World War such ideas were seen as increasingly delicate.

Intellectually, wherever possible, it was more desirable to dispense with invasions, and to attribute any cultural changes in Britain to trade and 'cultural transmission'. The 'Invasion Hypothesis', as it was termed, was heavily criticized in the 1960s. The ensuing purge left in the archaeological textbooks only a few settlements of people from the Continent in prehistory and no invasions proper.

Today it is no longer deemed necessary to explain the appearance of Continental styles of artefact by hostilities, indeed it is difficult to see why this idea should have gained favour, since the appearance of more far-flung artefacts (silk from China for example) was always seen as the result of trade rather than invasion. The post-war world, too, gave useful parallels as to how culture can be transmitted and assimilated without hostile invasion. The spread of American slang and fast-food restaurants in Britain, for example, has come about not through settlement or conquest but as an adjunct to viewing the USA as dynamic, successful, and emulatable. Similarly, French youth has adopted vast numbers of English words as a result of pop culture rather than 'invasion'. There is no reason to suppose that prehistoric cultures were not sometimes spread in a similar way, as part of a healthy trade in new, desirable commodities. The vendor offering iron goods for the first time would have found it easy to sell other commodities as part of a desirable package associated with progress and the future. Whatever language the seller spoke would have been seen as equally attractive.

Invasions are historically attested or claimed in the case of the Romans, Anglo-Saxons, Vikings, and Normans, so since 1945 attempts have been made to minimize their effects, partly by concentrating efforts on different, or sometimes new, types of evidence. The past fifteen years, for example, have seen the Anglo-Saxon settlements in particular reduced in the textbooks from large-scale settlements to the infiltration of small élites, with the corresponding survival of Romano-British patterns of settlement.

There is no doubt, however, that this, and similar exercises, have been based on more than cynical manipulation of the statistics. Interest in poorer Roman sites – ones that do not produce headline-worthy treasures or mosaics – has increased along with archaeological technology. Many thousands of sites have therefore been identified which were hitherto neither sought nor expected, and new techniques have often allowed reinterpretation of old excavations. Naturally, the perspectives have changed, not only enabling but positively requiring the scholarly re-think that was called for.

While there is little doubt that ideas of waves of invaders swamping the island population in prehistoric and early historic times is extremist, a detached observer might well feel that with Britain's proximity to Europe some degree of immigration is only to have been expected in the past.

Students of human nature might also suspect that not all these folk were possessed of smooth negotiating skills and charming personalities – some at least are likely to have taken by force what they wanted.

In times for which there are historical records for example, if unemployment is known to have been high, hostility to aliens has also usually been rife. In other periods the new skills or techniques have been welcomed as beneficial. In the sixteenth century the contribution of textile workers to England played a major role in the development of the cloth industry, and was tolerated despite growing unemployment, because of the benefits it bestowed. The migration to England of Flemings, Walloons, Dutch, and Huguenots (which was part of a wider pattern of refugee movements prompted by religious persecution on the Continent), led to the creation of large immigrant populations in the suburbs of London and in the East Anglian towns of Colchester, Norwich, and Ipswich. The colonies were often substantial – between the 1560s and 1618 the immigrant population in London had increased from 5,000 to 10,000, and by 1581 about a third of Norwich's population was Dutch or Walloon.

It is possible to study the relationships between the native and the immigrant population in historically documented societies, but this is difficult in earlier periods. As will be seen, the archaeological evidence in non-historic times can be interpreted in conflicting ways, perhaps indicating that this ambivalent attitude to incomers was always the case.

The subject of this book is vast but fascinating – an outline of some of the major European influences on Britain from the arrival of the first people to the Industrial Revolution (when the volume of material is too great to include). It is the argument of the book that Britain has always been an active participant in trends in European culture, and that the myth of British insularity is a product of the relatively recent past. Clearly the subject has to be painted with a broad brush, and as archaeologists and students of early art we confess to concentrating almost exclusively on material evidence.

The book is selective. For reasons of space we have chosen to discuss facets of the subject that seemed to us particularly illuminating, or for which archaeological evidence was particularly useful, or which demonstrated the scope and variety of the evidence. This has led inevitably to an emphasis on European trade with Britain, and to discussions of the extent of immigration from the Continent in antiquity. Some subjects, undoubtedly important in the dissemination of European culture, such as the medieval interest in pilgrimages, have barely been mentioned since the impact is difficult to assess in material terms, and some, such as the Crusades, were not included because the main arena lay outside Europe.

While writing the book we have become increasingly aware that it chiefly chronicles the lives of the rich, the poor of all periods being more likely to make do with homemade or locally produced goods. Generally however it is the features that permeated to the mass of the population which had the greatest long-term impact and which, interestingly, were probably not always regarded in high profile by their importers.

The book is not intended to be an academic treatise, even though academic matters keep breaking through into the narrative. Generally, it is intended to stimulate and, hopefully, divert. The reader will become aware that numerous topics in the early periods particularly, are surrounded by controversy – sometimes thousands of pages have been devoted to the debates. Archaeology is a strange subject in that it depends to a large extent on chance – what survives and what is discovered – and at the same time it enjoys some very precise scientific techniques for comparing and dating material. Frequently data appear conflicting until further evidence is forthcoming. As a result conclusions often rely on logic rather than hard and fast rules, a state of affairs that positively fosters fierce arguments and rival 'schools of thought'. These conflicting viewpoints are frequently equally valid at the time of being forwarded but the occasionally ferocious criticisms between colleagues and rivals add life and interest to the subject. The vast banks of data, sometimes unpublished and often obscure, also make it impossible for scholars to take into consideration every single particle of relevant information at any one time. The forwarding of theories and ideas is essential to the progression of the subject as workers in detailed areas can mull them over and pronounce as to their feasibility for their arena.

Fascinating though they all are, unless the arguments are directly relevant to the theme, we have often dealt with them somewhat summarily, and have included an extensive bibliography for those who wish to explore these areas further.

We are very much in debt to Philip Dixon, Jeffrey May, and Andrew Poulter, who all read sections of the text in a draft stage and gave much-appreciated advice, help, and suggestions.

CHAPTER ONE

Early Prehistory

THE BEGINNINGS OF BRITISH PREHISTORY

The first human inhabitants of Britain, about half a million years ago, must have been Palaeolithic immigrants from the Continent. Confusingly, however, the earliest human fossil in Europe is a limb bone from Boxgrove, West Sussex, found in 1994. It dates from around this time, as do recent finds of hand-axes from Waverley Wood, Warwickshire. The Channel was not yet formed, so it required merely stamina rather than technological or nautical skill to make the journey. To judge from the remains of 'Roger' (named after his finder at Boxgrove) these early people were of suitably stalwart physique: his remains initially imply that he was over six feet and a sturdy 13.5 stone. Prior to this find, the first fossil remains of ancestral modern man in Britain were found at Swanscombe in Kent dating from around 250000 BC.

Neanderthal fossils have been discovered at Pont Newydd in Clwyd, and have been dated to 225000 BC. The remains are much earlier than the majority of Neanderthal fossils in Europe, and perhaps represent an early stage in the development of the species. The Neanderthals must also have come from the Continent, and some Neanderthal teeth were found in Jersey, at La Cotte de Saint-Brelade.

During the last Ice Age, around 40000 BC, fully developed ancestors of modern man came to be the dominant species in Europe, and occupation in Britain was resumed after a gap when climatic conditions were severe. Habitation occurred almost exclusively in caves, and the associated tools are much more delicate that those of the preceding period, comprising elegant blades and antler objects, possibly used for straightening spear shafts, picturesquely named *bâtons de commandement*. The closest parallels for these assemblages are to be found in France.

There is virtually no evidence that Britain or the adjacent parts of France were occupied between about 25000 and 12000 BC, when the ice sheet had once more retreated leaving the whole of southern Britain available for settlement. People thereafter took the opportunity to come from the Continent in significant numbers, apparently occupying the same areas as their predecessors 1,400 years previously.

Around 6500–6000 BC, due to climatic changes, the English Channel was created, and thenceforth the Stone Age cultures developed mostly along their own lines.

FARMING – A CONTINENTAL INTRODUCTION

The next most significant introduction from the Continent was farming – and with it many features attendant upon a new way of life. The countryside gradually changed as the forests were cleared, roads were created, buildings replaced temporary campsites and the dead were revered with new burial rites and monuments.

Farming was developed independently at different times in different parts of the world, taking a journey from the Near East to Britain that lasted over 3,000 years. It crossed the Channel in the late fifth millennium BC and spread northwards. The precise methods by which it arrived – with immigrants or by cultural transmission – are debated.

The early British farming communities shared much in common with their nearest neighbours on the Continent, and they are all grouped together in archaeological studies as 'Western neolithic cultures'. From this period on it is possible to trace very clear links between specific areas of Britain and Europe.

The first such significant culture is that known as the Michelsberg, which was centred on modern Belgium. Michelsberg open, shouldered bowls with everted necks are very similar to pottery types found in eastern and northern Britain.

What is known as the TRB culture of Poland has been claimed to share links with both Michelsberg and the early British farming communities since all have common features, such as distinctive types of leaf-shaped flint arrowheads and the tradition of flint mining. Some scholars consider that

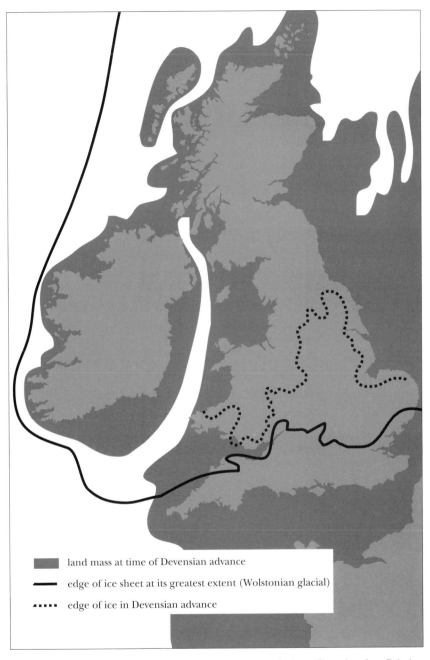

Map 1.   The Continental land mass in the Pleistocene, with the outline of modern Britain superimposed. (After L. Laing and J. Laing, Origins of Britain *(London, Routledge & Kegan Paul, 1980), Map 1.)*

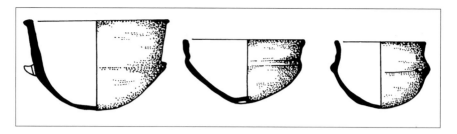

Fig. 1.   Neolithic pottery, British and Continental (left to right): Carn Brea, Cornwall; Michelsberg; Chassey.

the Polish TRB was ancestral to the Michelsberg, and that Michelsberg people crossed from Belgium to south-east England.

Brittany, too, had close ties with Britain – the pottery there is very close in design to that of south-west England, where it is known as the 'Hembury style'. Such pots have wide mouths and sharp shoulders, as well as lugs to aid lifting.

From this and other evidence, the new ideas associated with the Neolithic period must have spread from several points independently. Radiocarbon dates show farming being practised at Ballynagilly in Co. Tyrone at the end of the fifth millennium, and similar settlements seem to have been established between 4200 and 3500 BC at a diversity of locations in Britain from Scotland in the north to East Anglia and the Channel coast of England in the south.

Gastronomically, farming brought improvements. Once they had cleared land for cultivation, the farmers produced wheat and barley, and domesticated cattle, sheep, and pigs. A further addition to the diet is postulated by an interesting discovery made in a pit at Hambledon Hill, Dorset. Here the plant remains, which were dated by radiocarbon to around 4,500 years ago, included a grape seed. Not only is the seed from the earliest known grape in Britain, but if it is cultivated it is as early as any yet discovered in Europe, and raises the possibility that wine may have been another introduction from the Continent.

A major disadvantage of the new, European-style diet was the increase of dental caries.

BUILDING DEVELOPMENTS

It is significant in the development of humankind that farming facilitated and necessitated the growth of settled villages. This in turn marked the first steps towards the beginnings of civilization (the word is derived from the Latin *civis*: a citizen) – organized and cooperative human behaviour embracing larger units than the extended family or tribal group. People could now amass possessions (an activity which had not been practicable when they were constantly on the move following their food supplies), and, among other things, architecture could be developed.

Few early neolithic settlement sites are known in Britain. Where they have been found, they consist of houses rather than insubstantial shelters, and seem, on the whole, to have been much smaller than their counterparts on the Continent. A fairly substantial, rectangular timber building (with slots for foundation beams into which planked walling would have been slotted) was found at Fengate near Peterborough. Much larger rectangular halls were built later in the period. Authentic neolithic houses are modern tourist attractions at Skara Brae in the Orkneys where lack of wood necessitated the use of stone even for internal furniture.

Other architectural achievements are the so-called 'causewayed camps' – enclosures encircled by ditches broken by areas of undug ground or 'causeways', of which the most famous is that at Windmill Hill in Wiltshire. Although somewhat similar hilltop sites are found in the Michelsberg, they can be considered as a mainly British development.

The early farmers built timber corduroy roads, such as the Sweet Track in Somerset, and conducted a vigorous internal trade in both pottery and stone axes, many of which were produced from favoured stone at axe factories. Some fine examples were imported from Switzerland or the Alps. Made of jadeite they are clearly too fine and carefully made for use in clearing forests. One was found buried under the Sweet Track and others have been found in Wessex, East Anglia, and Scotland.

Another type of imported axe was made of Breton dolerite, and examples have been found concentrated near river mouths in southern England. Given the fact that axes are associated with ritual monuments in neolithic Britain (some were even carved out of chalk), it is likely they had an important magical or ritual significance, which seems to have persisted through prehistory. The fact that some of these ritual axes were imported suggests that the cult significance was also a Continental phenomenon. At the end of the third millennium BC Scandinavian flint axes and Baltic amber were being imported to Britain, and stone battle axes from central and northern Europe were both imported and widely copied.

COLLECTIVE BURIAL AND CHAMBERED TOMBS

A phenomenon found widespread in neolithic Europe including Britain is that of collective burial, most distinctively in graves built of massive stones – megalithic chambered tombs. It seems likely that these are the manifestations of religious beliefs which were shared in many parts of Europe. Undoubtedly, religious beliefs would have been modified simply because of the farming way of life – from now on different forces of nature would have been perceived to have been vital to well-being.

The many different types of collective tomb in Britain appear to represent indigenous developments on a regional basis, with two exceptions. It has been argued that the paved and roofed mortuary house, which is found occasionally in Britain, may have originated in Denmark, where examples occur in TRB contexts, for instance at Konens Høj and at Saltern. Secondly, one group of British stone-built tombs, with small chambers inside a square mound, on the Medway in Kent, are so close stylistically to the tombs of Denmark, Germany, and the Netherlands that the design may have emanated from these areas.

A notable feature of a series of impressive Irish tombs in the Boyne valley and some tombs in Orkney and Wales is the distinctive 'megalithic art', which is also encountered in France, particularly in the tombs of Brittany. The decoration includes abstract spiral and zig-zag patterns and also eye and eyebrow designs known as 'occuli'.

BEAKER PERIOD OR BEAKER PEOPLE?

The later Neolithic in Britain was characterized by the arrival of skills in copper and gold metallurgy. As with farming, copper working was not a single discovery in one place. Even in the Old World it seems to have been developed separately in three areas: Turkey, the Balkans, and Iberia. From the last two places the idea spread first inland in Europe and thence to Britain, enabling people to extend their tool kits.

Archaeologists argue animatedly over whether the third millennium BC saw an influx of immigrants or merely ideas and objects. Regardless of current changing opinion, the Beaker Folk, as they have been termed, are an essential part of the mythology of archaeology in Britain, and are associated with the introduction of copper working. In 1912 Lord Abercromby made a study of a distinctive class of pottery, and came to the conclusion that there had been an invasion to Britain from the Continent by the makers of distinct pots, which he termed Beakers. Associated with the pottery were new burial types, farming techniques – and metallurgy. Abercromby's simple 'invasion hypothesis' was later modified by a number of other scholars, who saw that the Beaker settlement of Britain was more complex. In the 1960s David Clarke postulated that there had been seven Beaker invasions or phases of settlement from the Continent, which gave rise to two different social systems, one northern and one southern. Others still can find no convincing arguments for actual movements of people.

Beakers are found widely through Europe, having been used in Scandinavia, Germany, the Low Countries, Spain, and Italy. Those that are closest in style to the British varieties have been found in the Netherlands, and it is fairly clear that it was from there that they first reached Britain, though whether as a result of immigration or through other forms of contact has been vigorously debated.

The most diagnostic features of 'Beaker Culture' in Britain are: the rite of single inhumations under round mounds or barrows, the use of metal, and the prevalence in the population of round skulls as opposed to the longer skulls of the earlier neolithic people. All these have been claimed as not intrusive but probably pre-existing features of late neolithic Britain. The change in skull shape, it has been argued, could have been the outcome of changes in the population in the previous centuries for which we have relatively little information about individuals or burial rites.

The first group of beakers in Britain are vessels with elegant, bell-shaped profiles, known as *all-over cord beakers* on account of their style of decoration. Despite some contra-indications, it is now generally felt that the

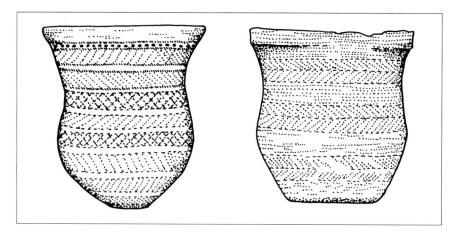

Fig. 2. Bell Beaker pottery, British and Continental. Left: Prague, Czechoslovakia. Right: Roundway, Wilts.

all-over cord beakers developed on the lower Rhine and in the Low Countries.

These early beakers have been found along the south and east coasts, notably the upper Thames valley, Salisbury Plain, East Anglia and the east coast of Scotland, which would be in keeping with either the idea of settlers or of cultural influence from the Continent.

The pots themselves were certainly status objects, perhaps more important on account of the liquid used in them. They may have been the equivalent of the Greek cups imported by the early Continental Celts from which to drink their imported wine, or the porcelain bowls imported into England from China in the eighteenth century for the consumption of tea. One beaker from Ashgrove in Fife was found to contain (extremely vintage) mead.

BEAKER BURIAL RITES

Burial rites are so different from the collective tombs of the preceding period that they are likely to represent a new set of beliefs or possibly social changes that brought about the aggrandizement of individuals – a concept of social structure that has remained, virtually continuously, to the present day. The earliest Beaker burials in Britain are typically found under a small circular mound of earth and stones, and usually consist of the remains of a single flexed body, sometimes accompanied by a copper dagger, copper pin, barbed and tanged arrowheads, and an archer's wrist guard of stone.

BEAKER METALLURGY

A notable feature of Beaker-period metalworking was the goldwork, not only basket-shaped ear-rings, but also splendid beaten gold necklets known as *lunulae* because of their crescent-moon shape. These are decorated with linear patterns reminiscent of beakers and are further evidence of the importance of certain individuals in the community. Gold 'sun-discs' may reflect cult interests.

Continuing links with the Continent are reflected in innovations in metal technology. By around 1800 BC the addition of tin to copper resulted in the development of bronzeworking. These new skills seem to have emanated from Saxo-Thuringia, although the methods by which they were disseminated to Britain are not clear.

BEAKER TRADE

As might be expected, trade flourished in the Beaker period. Analysis of a group of copper knives from Dorchester in Oxfordshire and Roundway in Wiltshire has shown that they were made from ore derived from central Europe. Another knife from Wiltshire can be demonstrated as having been made of Irish metal. Jadeite axes continued to be imported from the Continent, as was lava from the Niedermendig quarries in Germany, which were still supplying Anglo-Saxon England with querns nearly 3,000 years later. *Lunulae* were exported to the Continent.

THE WESSEX GRAVES

By the early second millennium BC, while beakers were still in use in the north of Britain, yet another cultural group with close Continental links evolved in the south, in Wessex. This, too, has been the centre of archaeological arguments. Rich burials, with sophisticated technology, and new types of pots and artefacts attesting far-flung contacts, suggest the development of a powerful aristocracy. Throughout the early twentieth century it was thought that the graves were those of an immigrant élite who grew rich through trade, particularly by controlling the flow of gold and other metal resources from Ireland through south Wales to the Continent, and through the parallel manipulation of a trade in Cornish tin.

However, archaeologists are increasingly of the view that the assemblages of artefacts represent an indigenous culture and that the real basis of the flourishing economy was pastoralism: trade being merely a reflection of prestige. Undoubtedly, as in other periods, immigrations took place partly to facilitate trade, but such movements need not be seen as 'invasions'.

Most of what is known about the Wessex aristocracy comes from their distinctive types of barrow, although they may also have been responsible for the building of the final phase of Stonehenge. The earliest of the Wessex burials were the richest. In some cases the graves were furnished with goldwork which must have been produced in Britain since it has no Continental counterpart, although European influence is apparent in some of the designs.

Much of the material assemblage found in Wessex graves seems to echo the local underlying Beaker traditions but, significantly, the most characteristic object (a flat dagger with a haft fastened on with six rivets), has its closest analogies in Brittany and Germany, where axes and arrowheads similar to those in Wessex graves have been found. Whether this is to be explained as a migration to Britain from Brittany, or vice versa, has been argued at various times in the past without conclusion.

It is now generally considered, however, that Brittany and Wessex were part of a single cultural pool, with traits derived from a third European source, the precocious bronzeworking culture of the Únêtice of central Europe. The flat dagger type may have originated in this area. Miniature versions of metal-shafted Únêtice halberds (daggers set at right-angles to the haft) have been found in Wessex graves. The Únêtice may also have been the source for Baltic amber which seems to have reached Wessex at this period. Although amber can sometimes still be picked up on the east coast of England, splendid objects such as the amber cup from Hove,

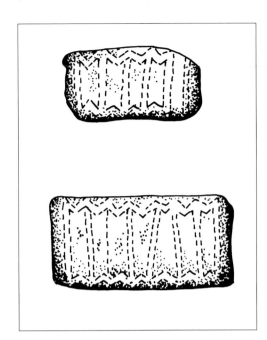

Fig. 3. Bronze Age amber necklace spacer-plates with complex perforations, British and Continental. Above: Upton Lovell, Wilts. Below: Kakovatos, Greece.

Sussex, are likely to have been imported. The occasional crutch-headed pins associated with Wessex burials are also Únêtice in style.

Additionally, the Wessex graves can be linked through trade to the east Mediterranean, where the Mycenaean civilization was flourishing in Greece. Some of the designs in Wessex goldwork are reminiscent of patterns found on objects from the Shaft Graves of Mycenae itself, but similar patterns are found widely in Bronze Age Europe and there need not be a direct link. On the other hand, gold-bound amber discs similar to some found in Wessex have been discovered at Knossos in Crete, and bone mounts thought to be from a ceremonial 'sceptre' from Bush Barrow in Wiltshire, are matched in grave Iota at Mycenae.

Similar in both areas, too, are amber necklaces with spacer-plates which have complex perforations for the threads. They are found at such sites as Kakovatos in Greece, where they are regarded as imports from Britain. Claims, too, have been made that an east Mediterranean dagger is among the carvings on Stonehenge, but this remains more doubtful.

Of particular interest are the beads of faience – blue glass frit – that have been found in some Wessex culture burials. These beads are of segmented and star-shaped form, identical to types found in the east Mediterranean, particularly Egypt. Although it has been suggested that they were made in Britain, or in central Europe (where similar beads are sometimes found), the diversity of the composition might argue against British manufacture. An east Mediterranean origin is likely since their manufacture would have required a highly developed and specialist technology.

Also found in Wessex contexts are putatively Cypriot ear-rings.

It is highly unlikely that there was any direct trade between Britain and the east Mediterranean, but objects from the area reached Britain (and vice versa) as part of a wider pattern of trade by which temperate Europe acquired objects from exotic southern civilizations.

Dating from the later Wessex culture is a fine gold cup from a burial at Rillaton, in Cornwall. The technology of this object (which is claimed to have held the collar studs of George V), employing as it does diamond-shaped washers, has led to claims that it was made in the Mediterranean. But this and similar vessels, one from Fritzdorf in Germany and another (of silver) from Brittany, are, on balance, more likely to have been local products.

The north of Britain and Ireland enjoyed a pattern of contacts with the Continent in the time of the Wessex graves which emphasized export rather than import. Northern British types of bronzework, for example, are found scattered through Westphalia and the Netherlands.

The Late Bronze Age – Another Invasion?

During the later part of the Bronze Age (from *c.* 1400 BC) Britain seems to have maintained a certain distance from her Continental neighbours. Even so, although settlements, economy, and pottery may have been distinctively British, the metalwork shows influence from north-west France, northern Germany, and probably Scandinavia.

Under nineteenth and early twentieth century thought, England experienced an invasion from the Continent in the later part of the Bronze Age of peoples who introduced a new burial custom: cremation in urns in unmarked cemeteries. These people, in Britain termed the 'Deverel–

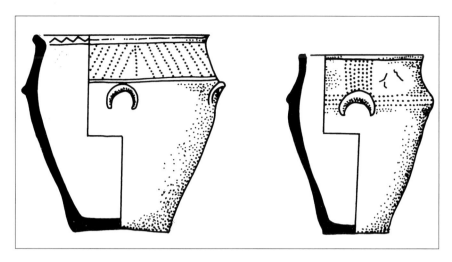

Fig. 4. Bronze Age urns, British and Continental. Left: Bulford, Wilts. Right: Budel, North Brabant.

Rimbury' culture (after two cemeteries), were seen to belong to the European 'Urnfield' culture that preceded the 'Celtic' cultures of Hallstatt and La Tène.

However, the period is difficult to interpret precisely, and with the discovery of radiocarbon dating it was possible validly to reinterpret the evidence by re-dating the Deverel–Rimbury people to the Middle or even the earlier Bronze Age. They were then seen as a parallel development with trends on the Continent.

From about 1450 BC there was a series of overlapping developments in bronzeworking. In the first two phases, called Acton Park and Taunton (after famous hoards), the metalwork in Britain is closely matched with that on the Continent, implying active interaction. The counterparts of the British products are found in France and Holland and the trade seems to have gone two ways – bar-twisted ornaments and composite tools were introduced from France, while Britain exported axes, ribbon torcs, and sheet metal. There are links also in pottery. Urns found in Wessex are very similar to pots known as Hilversum urns in Belgium, and pottery made in Cornwall known as Trevisker ware has been found at Hardelot in the Pas

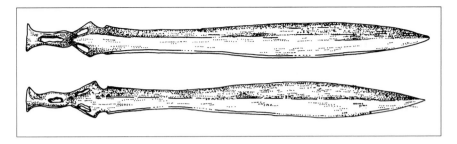

Fig. 5.   Late Bronze Age swords, 'Wilburton' type, British and Continental. Above: Kerguerou, Finistère. Below: River Thames, Battersea.

de Calais. Other features that link both sides of the Channel include burial customs – stake circles are found under burial mounds, and a rectangular building excavated at Martin Down, Dorset, can be paralleled on such sites in the Netherlands as Deventer.

The next two stages, which began about 1200 BC, are known after hoards as the Penard and Wilburton phases. This period, which extended until about 900 BC, saw the appearance of swords and new spear types which echo central European models. Wealth was displayed in the wearing of gold armlets and necklets. Beaten sheet bronzeworking resulted in the production of cauldrons, buckets, and shields – a technology which may have originated in the East Mediterranean and spread through Europe.

From 900 BC the final phase of the Bronze Age, known as the Ewart Park, was characterized by a new intensive period of bronzeworking. New types of weapons and edged tools for woodworking were developed, and from around 750 BC a variety of objects of types found in north-west France were commonplace in south-west England. In this period, too, pottery styles show changes reflecting Continental links – angular bowls were made in the tenth to eighth centuries BC, reflecting Continental styles.

During the eighth to sixth centuries BC a flourishing trade route operated along the Atlantic seaboard linking Iberia, France, and Britain. One of the most interesting facets of this was what appears to have been a common currency – small, socketed axes of distinctive types that are found in Britain and in north-west France in particular, where 315 hoards of metalwork were composed entirely of these objects, amounting to some 25,000 axes in all. These remained in use until the beginning of the iron-using phase and were usually too soft and small to have been useful tools, showing no sign of wear. As a form of primitive money, however, they make sense. Belonging to this Late Bronze Age phase, distinctive types of sword (known as carp's tongue swords) and cauldrons, once thought to originate in the Mediterranean but now seen to have been produced nearer home, were part of the trade represented by these axes. Many were made in Ireland and traded to England, Scotland, western France, and Denmark.

This settled development of Bronze Age life in Britain would presumably have continued indefinitely had not yet another European culture intruded – that associated with the Celts.

CHAPTER TWO

The Early Iron Age

WHO WERE THE CELTS?

The most enduring tradition from abroad is surely that of the Celts, who first made their appearance in the Late Bronze Age. Wales, Scotland, Ireland, the Isle of Man, and the south-west peninsula all claim to be Celtic, with varying degrees of fervour and meaning. There has been a tendency to regard the Celts as a people, united by a common language, culture, and belief system. In Continental Europe this has been equated with the spread of peoples from a homeland in south-west Germany, Czechoslovakia, and northern France. The picture now appears to be more complex than this, and the use of the term 'Celt' is often misleading, since it is sometimes used to mean 'speaker of a Celtic language' and sometimes to indicate 'a person belonging to a culture that is regarded as Celtic'.

The term is known only from historical sources, and was often used very loosely by Greek and Roman writers to describe European barbarians. Julius Caesar was clear that the Celts lived in what is now central and southern France, northern Italy, and probably south-west Germany. This is the key area in which a distinct archaeological culture, known as La Tène (after the type site in Switzerland, on Lake Neuchâtel), is found in the period from the fifth century BC onwards. From the central homeland, La Tène culture was originally seen by archaeologists to have spread outwards by either migrating or invading Celts. Two of the areas affected were seen to be Britain and Ireland, where among the new features claimed to have been introduced was Celtic language.

There is now a growing feeling that Celtic culture and Celtic language are not necessarily one and the same thing – some groups of people may have shared features of La Tène culture without speaking a Celtic tongue, and some Celtic speakers may not have adopted La Tène culture at all.

The situation in Britain is ambiguous. The population was never described by Classical writers as Celtic, but (to judge by Latinized versions of it) a Celtic language (or languages) was certainly spoken in the Iron Age. In archaeological terms, however, Britain seems to have been influenced by Continental La Tène culture.

It is no longer held probable that Celtic people arrived *en masse* in Britain to swamp the indigenous population. It is far more likely that the region embraced the culture which was common to much of Europe, and that in this wider context some movement of population occurred. What is notable about this change is its strength. Whereas cultural and trade links in the Wessex culture, for example, were confined to southern England, 'Celtic' influence eventually extended to encompass the whole of the British Isles including Ireland and the remotest of Scottish islands, where it remained to be later redefined and redeveloped in the Dark Ages. The tenacity of 'Celtic' culture in these areas, along with the restricted geographical extent of succeeding cultures in the south of England, is a factor that has contributed to the national differences within Britain itself – differences that led to the present Scottish, Welsh, and Irish nationalism.

THE CELTS ON THE CONTINENT

Celtic languages evolved gradually from earlier Indo-European roots, a process that was probably fairly erratic. What can be said is that an ancestral form of Celtic language was probably being spoken in the Late Bronze Age in central Europe; and it was in this region that two major Iron Age cultures of Europe grew up. Hallstatt, in the Austrian Salzkammergut, was the centre of a salt-mining industry, and this, along with growing technological skills, probably resulted in the emergence of a new warrior aristocracy.

The succeeding phase of European Celtic culture, the La Tène, emerged around the beginning of the fifth century BC, and its early phases coincide with a period of Celtic expansion which is well documented historically. It is also the period of an art style, which is one of the greatest glories of European civilization. The La Tène Celts traded with the Classical world, eventually sacking Etruscan cities, settling in northern Italy, sacking Rome and penetrating as far south as Sicily. In 279 BC they sacked Delphi. They settled in Turkey, and were employed as mercenaries in Mediterranean armies – a Celtic shield is among the finds from the Fayyum in Egypt.

From the third century BC onwards, however, the Celtic world began to shrink. Gradually the Romans encroached on Celtic territories, and finally, in 58–59 BC, Caesar's conquest of Gaul meant that the only remaining free 'Celtic' regions were Britain and Ireland. Caesar made two expeditions to Britain in 55 and 54 BC, but, despite considerable Romanization of the tribes of southern England, the area remained essentially Celtic until the Roman invasion of Claudius in AD 43. Even after this time, traditions survived more or less intact in the areas that lay beyond the frontiers of the province of Britannia.

Although Britain and Ireland were Celtic speaking, and possessed a 'Celtic' La Tène culture, there is no evidence of extensive settlement of invaders from the Continent, as was thought thirty years ago. The 'Celticization' of Britain was a subtle process, almost certainly the outcome of trade and ongoing contact rather than simple invasion. If Celtic were a language of trade, it would be easy to understand how it infiltrated even the most remote islands.

HALLSTATT CONTACTS AND TRADE IN BRITAIN IN THE SEVENTH TO FIFTH CENTURIES BC

Contact between Britain and Hallstatt Europe seems to have started in the seventh century BC, when long bronze and iron slashing swords became fashionable in the south of England, along with the winged chapes for their scabbards that enabled warriors to hold the scabbard down by foot while drawing the sword. Some imported swords of this type have been found in both Britain and Ireland, but they were soon copied. In the absence of any other evidence for immigrant warriors, it is now generally assumed that these objects were simply the result of early arms dealing.

During the seventh century BC a wide variety of objects, particularly harness and cart fittings, reached Britain. They have been found with indigenous objects in hoards: at Heathery Burn Cave in County Durham, and Welby in Leicestershire, where the finds included a bronze cup whose

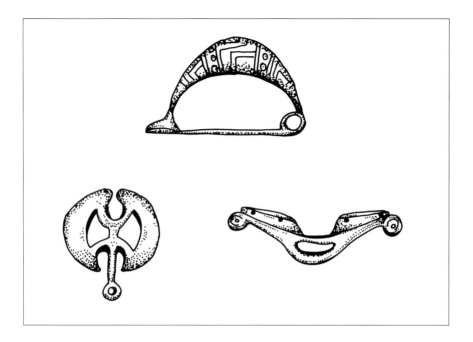

Fig. 6. Hallstatt imports in Britain. Top: brooch (restored), York. Left: razor, Midlothian, Scotland. Right: sword chape, Llyn Fawr, Glamorgan.

shape was imitated by British potters. Of particular interest is a hoard from Llyn Fawr, Glamorgan, which apart from local objects such as south-Welsh axe heads, socketed spearheads and sickles, contained a socketed iron spearhead, which could have been made either on the Continent or in Britain. Even more significantly, the hoard also contained a local type of sickle made of iron, an imported iron sword with bone side plates, and some Hallstatt harness mounts. The finds imply direct contact with the Continent, and the beginnings of local iron working. This evidence, along with other finds of Hallstatt harness fittings, suggests strongly that horses may have been imported.

It can be argued that all these high-status objects were likely to have been brought in by immigrants, but beside them were more mundane items which presumably reached Britain in the course of ordinary trade – pins, razors, and the like.

There was a lull in overseas trade in the sixth and early fifth centuries BC, although to this period belongs a ribbed bronze bucket from Weybridge, Surrey, similar to some found in rich Hallstatt graves. This, and a number of other objects, may have been diplomatic gifts. Also spanning the period from the eighth to the fourth centuries BC is a series of some eighty imported brooches. Many of them originated in Italy and were presumably traded through the Hallstatt and La Tène worlds of Continental Europe. Later Hallstatt and early La Tène objects seem to have entered the country by way of the Thames Valley – swords and daggers predominate. These were copied by British smiths. Actual imports are rare, and may well have been diplomatic gifts; some objects of more exotic origin in Italy and Greece dating from this time have been found in Britain, but how many are more recent losses rather than ancient imports is far from certain.

Northern Scotland, in particular Aberdeenshire, maintained close links with Germany in the later Bronze Age and Early Iron Age, to judge from objects from this region which were found in a hoard from Balmashanner, Angus. It has been postulated that there was some settlement in this region from the Continent.

BOATS AND SEAWAYS IN LATER PREHISTORY

The trade in bronzework in the Middle Bronze Age suggests strongly that there was a well-established pattern of seaborne activity involving Britain, Ireland, and France, which is likely to have have originated in an earlier period. By the first century BC, if not before, there were at least four main overseas trade routes.

The most venturesome travellers went from Ireland to the Continent, from Carnsore Point (Wexford) past the Scillies and Lizard Point to Ushant in Brittany. It has been calculated by Professor Sean McGrail that travel would have been at no more than 5 knots, and that to make the journey in daylight in summer would have involved being out of sight of land for at least ten hours, necessitating deep-sea navigational skills. It is additionally likely that sailing boats were employed in such voyages, as rowing would have been too demanding.

IMMIGRANTS TO BRITAIN IN THE FIFTH TO FOURTH CENTURIES BC

With the emergence of La Tène culture on the Continent, the trade links between Britain and Europe intensified. At this time there is more substantial evidence for settlement from the Continent. Some people may have come into eastern Yorkshire from the Marne region of France, introducing a distinctive burial practice involving the deposition of a two-wheeled vehicle in a square-ditched enclosure. There are many such burials in France, where the vehicles were the chariots of a warrior aristocracy, and were often richly furnished with exotic Greek imports and fine works of art. The English versions are more mundane, and most lack weaponry. Some imports are associated with the earliest, but most of them seem to date from very much later than the time of the Continental burials, and presumably represent a long-surviving tradition in Yorkshire where the early versions have not yet been discovered. The classic sites are at Arras, near Driffield, and Garton Slack.

Contact with the developing centres of La Tène power resulted in the appearance of angular pottery and new varieties of daggers in the area of the Thames, some very similar to their Continental prototypes. At this time the earliest imports of objects, decorated in La Tène style, can be distinguished, of which one of the earliest is an openwork disc from Danebury, Hants, similar to others from sites such as Somme-Bionne in France (from which there is a chariot burial). Two or three swords from the Thames seem to have been imports, perhaps from Switzerland and even Hungary. Safety-pin brooches are concentrated in central southern England, but few are imports though the British versions closely follow Continental trends in the fourth to second centuries BC. The brooches indicate that there was a period of active interaction between south-east England and her Continental neighbours in the later fifth and earlier fourth centuries BC, after which interplay was less vigorous.

BRITAIN AND THE MEDITERRANEAN, FIFTH TO SECOND CENTURIES BC

For the sixth century BC onwards, historical sources start to become increasingly important in a study of the British past, even though they do not always simplify matters. From this period, Britain came increasingly to

*Fig. 7. Iron Age coins of Cunobelin of the
Trinovantes, c. AD 40, with ship on reverse.*

the attention of the Mediterranean world – partly through trade and partly
because Roman power was expanding northwards. Mediterranean trade
probably came by way of a coastal route, round Gibraltar and northwards,
or by way of the Seine–Rhône, Loire–Rhône or the Garonne–Aude.

Trade with the Continent depends on easy Channel crossings, and by the
Iron Age there is plenty of evidence for sailing vessels. Caesar and Strabo
gave descriptions of the fleet of the Veneti of Armorica which plied the
Channel – the craft were plank-built, caulked with moss or reeds. Celtic
coins display representations of ships. A type of vessel known as a *ponto* in
Classical sources, which had a high stem projection, appears on coins of
the Continental Atrebates tribe and on coins of Cunobelin, who ruled in
south-east England just before the Roman Conquest. The Cunobelin coins
show a deep vessel with mast and square sail, and such ships may well have
been representative of a fleet which Cunobelin used to ply cross-channel
trade.

There is abundant evidence for hide boats in later prehistory. A gold
model from a hoard from Broighter, Co. Derry, dating from the first

century BC, is of just such a vessel, with nine rowing thwarts, three poles for propulsion in shallower water, and a yard on a mast. It would appear from Avienus that the ancestors of the Veneti were using hide boats for sea-going trade in the Bay of Biscay and western Channel, in the sixth century BC.

Britain was known to Classical writers as early as the sixth century BC. It was referred to as the island of the Albiones in the writings of Avienus (drawing on a sixth century source). Around the fourth century BC, the Greek traveller Pytheas visited Britain, his voyage perhaps prompted by stories told by tin traders returning to the Mediterranean.

Avienus wrote of Tartessians (from Spain) and Carthaginians (from north Africa) trading with Britain, apparently the south-west. Diodorus Siculus in the first century BC described how tin was obtained in Britain in the peninsula of Belerium, where it was fashioned into knuckle-bone shaped ingots and taken to 'an island which lies off Britain and is called Ictis'. The identity of Ictis has been debated; St Michael's Mount and Mount Batten, near Plymouth Sound, have been suggested, as has the Isle of Wight (Roman Vectis), in the hinterland of which there is, possibly significantly in this context, the largest distribution of Greek coin finds in Britain.

The archaeological evidence for the tin trade (and of Mediterranean trade in general) mainly comprises a very large number of finds of autonomous Greek coins in the British Isles, with concentrations in Dorset, Exeter and Sussex. Many of these, however, could have been lost in Roman times or even more recently by collectors, but there is growing evidence that a proportion reached Britain in the Early Iron Age. One coin of the Egyptian king Ptolemy V (204–181 BC), was associated with Iron Age British pottery in a pit at Winchester, Hants, and some Greek coins have been found on an Iron Age site in Kent.

A number of coins struck in Britain at the end of the first century BC and early in the first century AD have types based on Greek coins. What is notable is the fact that the suggested models are frequently of much earlier date than the Celtic derivatives, a significant number being of the fourth and third centuries BC. Additionally, some prototypes seem to be coins which were intended for a local token currency, such as the bronze issues of Aitna in Sicily, struck in the second century BC, that provided the reverse design for a coin of Cunobelin.

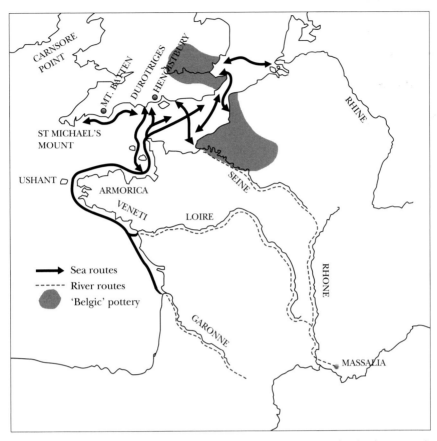

Map 2. Southern Britain and Continental trade routes in the later Iron Age (various sources).

A further clue to the existence and extent of Mediterranean trade is the occurrence of Gaulish imitations of the coins of Massalia (Marseilles) that have been found in southern and midland Britain. Not all of these were produced in the immediate hinterland of Marseilles, but they seem to have given rise to British copies. The closest are known as 'Thurrock' bronzes after a site in Essex where a large hoard was reputedly found. They are common in both Essex and Kent, and date from at least the early first century BC. A second series is very much cruder, but of comparable date, and again is concentrated in the south-east. They comprise the earliest coins minted in Britain, and underline the important fact that coinage was an introduction to Britain from the Continent.

Fig. 8. Cast bronze or 'potin' imitations struck in Britain of Massaliote types. Above: 'Thurrock' type. Below: 'heavy striations' type of Kent.

A remarkable discovery in Ireland has added a new dimension to the study of Mediterranean links with Britain in the Early Iron Age. At the ritual site of Navan in Co. Armagh the skull of a barbary ape was found in a context which was dated by archaeological means to around 250–100 BC, corroborated by radiocarbon dating centred on 200 BC. Taken along with the find of a boat from Lough Lene, which has Mediterranean features, it has been deduced that this points to a trade between Ireland and Carthage in the later first millennium BC.

The Atlantic trade with the south-west in the Iron Age is further supported by the discovery at Harlyn Bay, Cornwall, and Mount Batten, Devon, of fifth-century BC brooches of a distinctive type found in Spain and south-west France.

THE ROMAN CONQUEST OF GAUL

The development of trade in general with Britain in the first century BC was furthered by Roman activities in southern Gaul, and the foundation of the Roman colony at Narbonne. Eventually Caesar established Roman power as far north as Belgium, Holland, and the south-west bank of the Rhine. It would appear that the Gallic tribes paid British mercenaries for their support, a fact which may be reflected in the very large number of gold coins minted at this time on the Continent, that are scattered through Britain. Some of these seem to have been melted down to provide the raw material for native British issues. Thenceforth, the Atlantic trade with southern Gaul and the Mediterranean was eclipsed by a more direct route connecting northern Gaul and south-east England. Further west, a vigorous trade continued to link Dorset and adjacent areas with Armorica.

The general picture in the late first century BC was one of expanding trade links, and among the commodities sought by the Celts was wine, for which they offered slaves and metals, among them no doubt tin.

A key site in understanding British trade with Gaul at this time is Hengistbury Head in Dorset. Already in the first half of the first century BC Mediterranean wine amphorae, Armorican pottery, figs, and lumps of glass were arriving there, to be traded for iron, Kimmeridge shale, salt, gold, copper, tin, lead, and probably grain. The trade route for which Hengistbury was the terminus probably started in northern Italy, and went via Narbonne, the Carcassonne gap, the Gironde, the Atlantic coast of France, and the Solent. Poole harbour nearby may have been another point of trade.

From the Dorset coast amphorae of wine are known to have been taken 50–60 km inland, and Armorican coins spread out even further. To judge from Caesar, much of the trade was in the hands of Venetic merchants. In 56 BC, he sank their fleet and, together with the concomitant damage Roman forces inflicted on the other Armorican tribes, effectively put an end to this trade. Pottery from Brittany ceased to appear in archaeological levels at Hengistbury, and wine amphorae became correspondingly rare. The trade between the south-east and Gaul, however, was not much affected by the vicissitudes of fortune in Armorica. From the middle of the first century BC fine Roman merchandise, including wine amphorae, bronze vessels for the consumption of wine, glass, and Augustan silver cups flowed steadily into the region.

CHANGES IN BRITISH LIFESTYLE

While the Romans were gradually consolidating their presence in Gaul, the southern British countryside was changing – no doubt as a response to the increasingly sophisticated way of life facilitated by the new trade links and ideas. Until the first century BC the dominant features in some areas of the Iron Age British landscape were the hillforts. They were focal points in a primarily agricultural landscape, and served two main functions, as centres from which raiding could be carried out and as distributive foci for merchandise and food surpluses.

As trade with the Continent intensified in the mid-first century BC, hillforts went into decline in the southern chalklands, to be replaced by a different type of nucleated settlement. Archaeologists today have adopted, perhaps unwisely, the Latin term *oppidum*, literally 'a town', for such sites. These were sited on low-lying ground, and comprised tracts of land defined by banks and ditches. British *oppida* are characterized by their mints and by the relative abundance of imported pottery from northern Gaul and from further afield. The key points for control were now places situated on the trade routes that were vital both for internal distribution and the marketing of foreign produce.

The southern British were closely connected with the Continent in several ways. Caesar, for example, wrote of a king called Diviciacus of the Continental Suessiones who ruled on both sides of the Channel sometime before the mid-first century BC. It is notable that two of the series of early gold coins found in Britain were characteristic of the region of Gaul occupied by the Suessiones tribe – from which Diviciacus came. It is also notable that coins in one of the series associated with the Suessiones (which have a triple-tailed horse on the reverse), although extremely rare as imports in Britain, nevertheless gave rise to a major series of British copies. This suggests that the Continental prototypes had a political or cultural significance for the southern Britons, far in excess of their commercial importance.

THE 'BELGIC INVASION'

The story of the first century BC and early years of the first century AD is extremely shadowy, despite the few Classical written records. Attempts to illuminate it have been made, using a combination of historical evidence and clues provided by archaeology. Of these, the most important take the form of coins, the later issues of which were inscribed with the names of rulers, and in one case with the name of a tribe – the Iceni of East Anglia. Inconveniently for scholars, the tribes mentioned by Caesar do not seem to have survived in name until the Roman Conquest under Claudius, but, nevertheless, the distribution of uninscribed gold coins shows patterns which seem roughly to coincide with the later tribal divisions of Britain as known from Roman writers.

Caesar asserted that the coastal region of Britain was 'inhabited by immigrants from Belgium who came to plunder and make war – nearly all of them retaining the names of the tribes from which they originated – and who later settled down to till the soil'. This categorical statement of hostile invasion is not universally accepted, however, since it is not incorporated into Caesar's main text, so once more debate over 'invasions' surrounds a period of undoubted Continental influence.

Sir Arthur Evans first drew attention in the late nineteenth century to the close similarities between wheel-thrown pottery in a cemetery at Aylesford in Kent and Late Iron Age pottery on the Continent. Since then there has been a persistent tradition in British archaeology to equate wheel-thrown pottery with Caesar's invasion from 'Belgium' and settlement of south-eastern Britain. It was pointed out that throughout the region could be found similar wheel-made, cordoned pottery in distinctive shapes, such as elegant urns with raised pedestal bases, a gold coinage directly inspired by Continental prototypes and new burial and possibly farming practices, attributed to the introduction of the 'Belgic plough' (the latter now regarded as a fiction). It was argued with varying degrees of credibility that these innovations must have been due to the arrival of immigrants from what the Romans knew as Gallia Belgica (an area which partly coincides with modern Belgium), and that the incomers set about controlling the tribes of the south-east while maintaining close links with their Gaulish homelands.

The arrival of the Belgae was for long seen to be coincidental with the appearance of gold coins in Britain, and a date for these was set at around 75 BC. This was also seen as the date for the earliest cemeteries with 'Belgic' pottery.

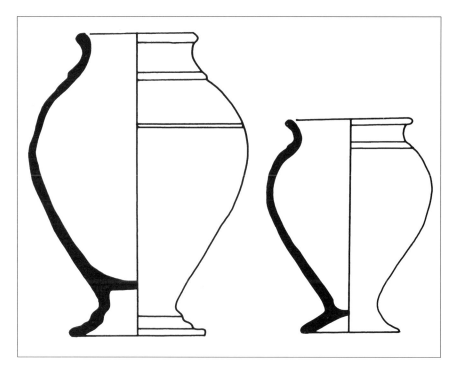

Fig. 9. 'Belgic' pottery, Continental and British. Left: Montepreux, Marne. Right: Aylesford, Kent.

By 1960, however, numismatists were dating some of the coins as early as 150 BC, and were arguing in favour of a series of invasions from Gaul, starting with people of the tribe of the Ambiani and followed by people from the Bellovaci, the Atrebates and then the Morini, whose coins were also widely distributed in the south-east. A considerable body of opinion now favours the view that although the coins were imports, they do not represent any actual settlement of people, and the original tribal attributions have been modified. Instead, they are seen as status objects intended for use in diplomatic gift exchange. The first issues probably arrived during the last years of the second century BC and these early gold coins were being copied in Britain before the middle of the first century BC, the earliest copies being quite close to the originals. In due course silver and then bronze coins were struck, and this seems to signal a shift from their being commodities used in gift exchange to their use in regular trade.

None of the distinctive wheel-thrown pottery seems to date from before the middle of the first century BC, but it is possible that its appearance in the south-east may be explained by a small influx of warrior aristocrats who took over at the top in the way that the Anglo-Saxons and Normans did later. It has been suggested that the focus of the Continental settlement lay in Hampshire and Sussex, where in Roman times a tribal group known as the Belgae was located. Their capital was at Winchester (Venta Belgarum). Under this viewpoint, the original settlement was reinforced around the middle of the first century BC by further immigrants, led by Commius of the Continental Atrebates, who was forced to flee from Caesar (whom he had formerly helped) to take refuge among the Atrebates in Hampshire.

It has been suggested that Caesar viewed the Atrebates of Hampshire/Sussex as a useful buffer between the more hostile Durotriges of Dorset (who were the former trading partners of the tribes of Armorica) and the inhabitants of the region he had targeted as his landing point. This might explain the flow of gold into Atrebatic territory.

In essence, the impact of Caesar's two brief British campaigns served to highlight the division between the more Gaulish and Roman-influenced regions of south-eastern Britain, which comprised the Atrebates, the Cantii of Kent, and the Catuvellauni/Trinovantes of Hertfordshire and Essex, and the fringe areas beyond. In the south-east the Trinovantes/Catuvellauni, influenced more by Rome, started introducing design elements in their coins borrowed from Roman denarii, and started striking coins in silver. Their neighbours soon followed suit.

Perhaps occasioned by the flight of Commius, a common cultural province seems to have grown up on either side of the Channel, sharing similar types of pottery, burial rites, and trade goods. These strongly reflect that the trade was Rome-driven; dominant in the trade assemblage are articles associated with that most celebrated Roman status activity, wine drinking.

As Roman control and influence in Gaul deepened, particularly during and after the reign of Augustus (from 27 BC), the traditional links between

British and Gaulish leaders were superseded by direct trade and diplomatic links with the Roman world. The main recipients of Roman favour seem to have been the tribespeople of Hertfordshire and Essex, since this is where the densest concentrations of Roman imports are found. Increasingly in the south and eastern region and in the territory of the Atrebates, coin types have been found, directly modelled on Roman issues. These sometimes displayed portraits of Augustus and Tiberius.

Writing about the trade situation in Britain in general in Augustus' time, Strabo listed the main exports of Britain to the Roman world as wheat, cattle, gold, silver, iron, hides, slaves, and hunting dogs. In addition, pearls and tin were probably exported. The imports he designated as bracelets, necklaces, amber, and glassware. Somewhat surprisingly, these commodities do not figure much in the archaeological record of Iron Age Britain, although the glass may have been melted down to rework into enamel or into native types of beads or even playing pieces, such as were found in a burial at Welwyn Garden City, Herts.

Tribal struggles for supremacy continued until about 10 BC, when there are signs of anarchy. Significantly, at this time Tincommius and Dubnovellaunus, rulers of the Atrebates and Trinovantes respectively, fled to Rome to seek help and protection from Augustus.

By the early first century AD the political situation in Britain had stabilized, and Cunobelin of the Trinovantes emerged as the most powerful ruler in the south-east. His capital was the oppidum of Camulodunum (near Colchester), defended by a system of earthworks. It soon flourished as a trading post, importing Italian Arretine and south Gaulish samian pottery, fine red gloss *terra rubra* and black gloss *terra nigra* pottery from Gaul. Roman and Gaulish coins were in use as well as native British. Here too, to judge by the graffiti on pottery, literacy penetrated, although growing literacy through contact with the Roman world is especially apparent from the increasing use of inscriptions on coins of the later first century BC.

On the eve of the Claudian invasion in AD 43 the aristocracy of the south-east had become thoroughly 'civilized'. The Romans called them 'barbarians', but compared to many modern Britons, the rich lived well. A series of burials from Essex and Hertfordshire show just how much

Romanization had made an impact on the Britons. The burials such as those from the Welwyn area, Herts, and a recent find at St Albans, are furnished with amphorae from the Falernian area of Italy. Silver cups of Augustan manufacture were found at Welwyn, and a grave at Lexden near Colchester included imported bronze statuettes manufactured in Gaul to Roman taste. Other finds, such as the bronze bust of Caligula found near Colchester and a pendant made with a bust of Augustus modelled on a Roman coin from Lexden, show that taste for Roman art did not stop with borrowing it for coins. Southern Britain was ready for a whole new lifestyle from Mediterranean Europe.

CHAPTER THREE

The Romans in Britain

From AD 43, for nearly four centuries, through Roman culture, the impact of Europe on Britain was incalculable, since for the first time the centre of power that controlled many tribes lay on the Continent. In addition, despite the strength of local and regional administrations, power lay in the hands of people who spoke a 'foreign' language. Insularity was no longer possible nor desirable. The focus of attention in Britain had previously been primarily intertribal, but now the emphasis was increasingly on the relationship of Roman Britannia with Rome. There was an emphasis on defending the area against other tribes outside the Roman boundaries. For nearly four centuries Britain lay at the western and northern limit of an advanced European civilization which stretched from Syria in the east to north Africa in the south, a civilization which, though still retaining some regional characteristics, nevertheless imposed similar values and cultural aspirations throughout all the territories over which it held sway. The Roman world was militaristic, bureaucratic, and literate, with good communications; in many ways it was the antithesis of the barbarian cultures it enveloped.

Unlike any previous influx of people from the Continent over which archaeologists argue, the Roman appearance in Britain was a genuine, aggressive, historically attested invasion. Control was established through pitched battles and the foundation of fortresses and forts at strategic points. Once an area was subdued effectively the armies moved northwards and westwards.

Although the Romans reached northern Scotland and, to judge from one Roman-style grave found in 1852, may even have travelled to Ireland, for most of the period the northern boundary was Hadrian's Wall. For a brief interlude the Forth–Clyde line (the Antonine Wall) was defended but soon abandoned.

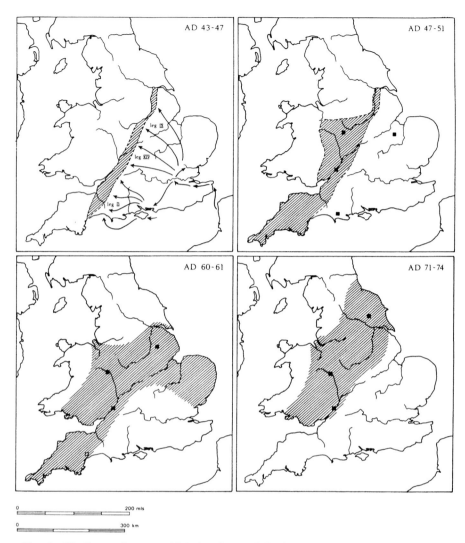

Map 3.   The Roman Conquest of Britain. (Source: B.W. Cunliffe, Iron Age Communities
of Britain *(London, Routledge, 1991), map Fig. 10.3.)*

By the end of the first century AD, there were two distinct zones within
Britain, a heartland, comprising the highly Romanized 'civil' zone, and the
periphery, or 'military' zone, where Romanizing influence on the native
population was more superficial, if brutal. Beyond this, in the regions
outside the province, particularly in Scotland, the influence of Rome was

less immediate but none the less affected the development of native Celtic culture. Roman merchandise penetrated far into the Highlands and Islands, and chiefs chose to be buried with Roman items as status symbols. Roman glass and pottery has been found on native sites as far north as Orkney, and a Roman clay model of a bale of sheepskin has been found in the Hebrides.

Britain, already exporting heavily the items listed by Strabo, was a desirable prize. To his original list of exports others can now be added, including ornaments in Whitby jet, and, in the late Roman period, the famous *byrrus Britannicus* (a kind of duffel coat). In the late third century a panegyric addressed to the emperor Constantius Chlorus described Britain as a 'land with such a wealth of fruits, rejoicing in such a number of pastures, abounding in veins of ores, so profitable in its revenues, surrounded by so many harbours, so vast in its circuit'. Even in the post-Roman fifth century, when Roman administration had broken down and trade links were severely curtailed, it was seen as a 'most wealthy island'.

Desire for such riches led to vast changes in everyday life with the new European influence, although there is no doubt that the greatest changes occurred in the lives of the rich and prosperous.

ADMINISTRATION

Romanization did not lead to the total extinction of native culture. Not only would it have been impossible to eradicate all things barbarian, but there were positive advantages in not doing so. The basic administrative structure of Roman Britain remained rooted in the traditional tribal areas. Where in the Iron Age there had been oppida and hillforts as tribal foci, now there were towns to take over the same functions and extend them. In some cases the towns were on the sites of their Iron Age predecessors – as for example at Calleva Atrebatum (Silchester), built on the site of the Atrebatic oppidum. Where the traditional site was potentially a focus for insurrection, or perhaps simply inconvenient, a new location was found – thus Durnovaria (Dorchester, Dorset), replaced the Iron Age fortress of Maiden Castle. Some towns were created through deliberate military action, the army handing over former fortresses to civilians, in some cases even helping them to lay out municipal buildings, as at Wroxeter, Salop, or constructing houses as in Verulamium. Some settlements were deliberately founded for inhabitants from the ranks of retired legionaries whose loyalty to Rome and a Roman way of life was indisputable. An early example of such a 'show' *colonia* is Colchester. Civilian settlements grew up round military sites, and some later superseded them, for example at Great Casterton (Rutland) or Dorchester (Oxon).

Within this urban structure the law was administered; minor matters were still subject to old tribal law, provided it did not conflict with Roman, rather as local by-laws operate in Britain today. Major judicial matters were a concern for higher authority, administered through various levels of courts up to that of the governor in London or ultimately the emperor in Rome. The legal system itself was an important method of spreading Roman values.

The Roman historian Tacitus stated that town growth stemmed from the educational policy of the general Agricola. He claims that this was responsible for the spread of such varied features of European taste as dress-style, porticos, bathing establishments, and dinner parties.

The new lifestyle demanded buildings never seen in Britain before. Public and private baths (complete with the new concept of latrines), fora, and municipal buildings, as well as theatres and amphitheatres for organized public entertainment gave a whole new dimension to leisure-time. Towns were laid out on similar lines to those in Gaul, though with subtle differences. Municipal baths, for example, were originally uncovered, but the exigencies of the weather soon led to these being roofed.

In 122 Hadrian visited Britain, and prompted a programme of civic building. Town buildings were replaced in stone at around this time. No doubt the original wooden buildings were decaying, but the permanence of stone also displays self-confidence, a determination to stay, and economic wealth. During the second century municipal building in stone progressed apace, as did the trade links and general prosperity of the province. The most lasting effect of the towns has been their siting – despite some misfortunes during the post-Roman period, large numbers are still in existence today. At the hub of the trade network lay Londinium, originally a Celtic foundation but developed in the Roman period and so strategically placed that it became, as it has remained, the foremost city.

PLACENAMES

Many hundreds of Roman period placenames are known from written sources, but very few have survived to the present day. Two of the best known are Vindolanda and Verulamium, the names of which have been revived as a result of archaeological excavations. Some pre-Roman placenames are known from Roman sources, for example Camulodunum (Colchester) which is referred to by Ptolemy (*c.* 140) as Kamoudolanon. London has changed hardly at all since it was mentioned as Londinium by Tacitus in AD 115–117 and may derive from a personal name or a tribe. Names are known from Classical sources such as the *Geography of Ptolemy*, the *Antonine Itinerary* (*c.* AD 220) or the *Ravenna Cosmography* (seventh century, but using no post-Roman material). It is not always possible to identify the place concerned, and sometimes the wrong identification is known to have been made. Recently discovered written evidence from Vindolanda, for example, makes it clear that the Roman name for Corbridge was Coria not Corstopitum. Lincoln is one of the few placenames to survive at least in element – from *Lin*dum *Colo*nia. Catterick has an ancient derivation, being known first from Ptolemy as Katouraktonion. It is probably a Briticized form of Latin *cataracta*, a waterfall. York has changed by degrees from Eboracum. Latin elements in placenames seem to have been adopted by the Britons – foss (ditch), port (port and gate), and caester (fort) – and have passed into English through this medium. Thus we have Chester, Manchester, and so on, and Portsmouth, Catfoss, and Foss Dyke. Sometimes words used by the Anglo-Saxons to denote Roman remains are still used, of which an outstanding example is *street*, which often refers to an old Roman road.

The majority of Latinized names (e.g. Brompton Regis, Toller Porcorum, the many Parva and Magna suffixes and other Latinizations) very considerably post-date the Roman period and are not survivals.

COMMUNICATIONS

One of the major ways in which Roman life has affected even the present day was road building. Some roads, such as the A5, are still major arterial routes, although many are concealed by numbers – the aliases of the Fosse

Way include the A46, the B4029, and the A429. Some remains of road building are still visible, of which the most spectacular example is at Blackstone Edge near Preston (Lancs).

Waterways were also important, and Dover, with its remarkably well-preserved lighthouse, was one of the main harbours for cross-Channel trade, whence goods travelled to the Seine, Garonne, and Loire.

THE COUNTRYSIDE

In the countryside, Roman farmsteads gradually replaced Iron Age ones in the civil zone. Villa is a term that can describe anything from a large bailiff-run estate that carried out a variety of economic functions, to the rural home of a Romano-British farmer, or the luxury home of a rich person.

Some Britons, particularly in the Belgic south, took to the Roman lifestyle easily – this is well exemplified by the palace discovered at Fishbourne, Sussex, built around AD 75–80. It flourished until the last years of the third century and was based on a Mediterranean model, laid out round a court with an impressive entrance which led through gardens to the audience chamber. Its floors were inlaid with over twenty of the finest mosaics in the current mode – shaped tiles, or *opus sectile*, black and white mosaics in geometric designs, and even mosaics with minute cubes or tesserae known as *opus vermiculatum*, similar to those found at Pompeii and Herculaneum. The walls were painted in fashionable style – one painting was similar to a harbour scene at Stabiae in Italy. Foreign craftsmen must have been brought in to create the decor. The identity of the owner is unknown, but Cogidubnus, king of the Regnenses and ally of Rome, has been suggested as likely. In common with other rich villas, Fishbourne was centrally heated by the late first century – another concept new to Britain.

Such splendid edifices were, however, the exception rather than the rule, especially until the fourth century, when a series of sumptuous villas, typically in the south and south-west, were built or refurbished. Of these North Leigh (Oxon), Chedworth (Glos.), Low Ham (Somerset) and Woodchester (Glos.) are particularly noteworthy. Such properties required considerable prosperity to build, maintain, and run, and during the second and third centuries less spectacular villas were built, of which Park Street and Lockleys in Hertfordshire are good examples.

Stone-built villas were rare until after AD 200, the date when stone building commenced at Bignor, Sussex.

The development of villas was gradual – normally traditional-style farms were refurbished or modified as time went on and money allowed. They differ from their forerunners in plan – rectangular rooms and layouts rather than round being the most definitive feature. There were a number of different plans (originally developed for the Mediterranean climate) – the courtyard villa and the winged corridor villa to name two examples. The uniformity of plans has allowed identification from aerial photography of increasing numbers in the past few decades. Layout is significant in that it implies a different lifestyle. Bedrooms, kitchens, bath buildings, dining rooms, and atria all required a rethink of everyday living that would not be possible without embracing new attitudes and values.

Gardens were a feature of large villas, and probably of less sumptuous ones, but it is notable that they have been ignored or wrongly identified by early excavators, who often preferred to find a prosaic function for a path – to a sheep pen rather than through an arbour or to a pergola. The Romans were, as far as evidence allows at present, the first people to introduce to Britain the idea of a pleasure garden (as opposed to a small enclosure given over to food production, which can be inferred, but not proved, in prehistoric times). Wall paintings from all over the empire abound with depictions of trellis, flowers, pergolas, and water in gardens, and there is no doubt that the art of pleasure gardening was highly developed. The most extensively excavated Roman garden that was identified as such at the time of excavation is at Fishbourne. Here the gardener was faced with a problem common to all creators of brand-new gardens when the builders have left – unproductive soil. In order to support what were probably box hedges, trenches were cut out and filled with rich soil.

What little other evidence there is for Roman gardens sounds very familiar – at Frocester (Glos.) in the early fourth century box hedges were grown and a driveway was edged with turf verges into which rectangular flower beds had been cut. At Rockbourne in Hampshire the horticulturalist had created a square walled garden with a pond. New flowers introduced by the Romans included roses, lilies, pansies, violets, and poppies, all standard features of modern gardens. And it is known from the discovery of pips and stones that grapes, sweet cherries, and plums were grown.

Purely native-style farmsteads continued to exist, displaying a greater or lesser degree of Romanization. Some, such as Woodcutts or Rotherley on Cranborne Chase, Dorset, remained essentially Iron Age farms using some Roman merchandise, others went further and had the other amenities of civilized life, such as wall paintings or paved floors.

In the military zone, deliberate Roman planning sometimes resulted in the replacement of earlier timber-framed huts with stone-walled hut groups. A Welsh response to villa architecture can be seen in the rectilinear planning at Din Lligwy on Anglesey. This was otherwise essentially an Iron Age-style establishment.

The introduction of new farming techniques was probably of greater significance to the average Romano-British country person than expensive new houses. Agriculture was improved by a plough with a coulter in front and a heavy iron bar share. An iron-tipped spade and a rake and scythe were also introduced. Giant 7 ft (2.1 m) hand scythes are known from Great Chesterford (Essex) and Barnsley Park (Glos.). New crops included oats, rye, vetch, flax, cabbage, parsnip, turnip, celery, carrot, vines, apple, mulberry, and walnut. The legacy of the Roman period to the modern gardener and cook is clearly considerable, although not all of these crops have necessarily been in continuous production since the Roman period.

Probably the greatest lasting impact on the landscape effected in Roman times was the drainage of the Fens. The intensive settlement of the Fenland of East Anglia began around AD 120, when a major influx of people to the area was accompanied by the construction of waterways, roads, and long-distance boundaries. These must have been the result of official policy to increase resources to the army. The exploitation of the region involved the digging of such canals as that known now as Car Dyke in Cambridgeshire and Lincolnshire. The operation was not totally successful, for catastrophic flooding devastated the region in the mid-third century.

THE POPULATION OF ROMAN BRITAIN

The invading Claudian army comprised around 40,000 men but it is almost impossible to determine how many civilians were also involved in the immediate follow-up of the conquest. They would have been heavily outnumbered by the native population. By the end of the Roman period, tentative estimates have suggested that the total population might have been in excess of 4 million. These estimates naturally include people whose way of life (in the rural areas) probably differed very little from that of their pre-Roman ancestors. Subsistence living or self-sufficiency leaves little scope for luxuries or the finer aspects offered by civilization. It also notoriously requires few durable materials, thus leaving little data for accurate statistics.

The movement of people in the Roman Empire is documented through, among other sources, inscriptions – particularly tombstones. Not surprisingly, many of the people so commemorated in Britain came from Gaul or Germany, but quite a few seem to have come from Greece or Syria.

A tombstone of a lady from South Shields reveals that she was married to a Palmyrene (from the trading city of Palmyra in Syria). Not only does her memorial carry an inscription in Palmyrene letters, but it is executed in Palmyrene style, suggesting that her husband had a sculptor in his entourage. A Greek doctor was buried in Chester.

Military tombstones are the most informative – at Wroxeter a soldier from the Fourteenth Legion had come from Vicenza; one from the Ninth Legion at Lincoln came from Heraclea in Greece; an auxiliary buried in Cirencester hailed from Augst, on the Upper Rhine, one from Gloucester came from Thrace (now Bulgaria); a soldier from the Second Legion at Lincoln came from Hungary. Buried at Caerleon, in South Wales, Gaius Valerius Victor is reported on his tombstone as having been born at the city of Lugdunum (Lyons). Unofficial liaisons with British women can be taken for granted as well as official marriages that took place on discharge from the army. Within a few years of the conquest the population mix would have been very considerable. Written evidence proves the existence in Britain of troops from all over the Empire – the Second Legion came from Strasbourg, the Twentieth from Neuss, the Ninth from Pannonia (on the Danube), and the Fourteenth from Mainz. Among the individual units

mention may be made of the Syrian archers on the two walls in the second
century, a unit of Frisians at Housesteads on Hadrian's Wall in AD 222–35, a
unit from the Tigris based on first Lancaster then South Shields, and a unit
from Spain at Llanio in Wales, to take a few examples.

Conversely, British soldiers are commemorated in various parts of the
Empire from Africa to Raetia.

Another type of evidence relates to a six-year-old Greek child who died
and was buried at Poundbury in Dorset. When analysed, four skeletons
from the cemetery were found to have absorbed large quantities of lead,
presumably from using lead or pewter dishes. The analysis of the lead from
three of the burials indicated it had been mined in the Mendips, but the
lead from the child did not match any British source and could only be
paralleled at Laurion, in Attica. Of course, the infant might have been fed
exclusively from Greek tableware!

The cosmopolitan character of Roman Britain is perhaps nowhere as
clearly seen as in the inscriptions found at Bath. Then, as now, a spa town,
Roman Aquae Sulis was famous for the healing properties of its spring. It is
likely to have been a fashionable resort, popular with holidaymakers as well
as the sick. In the first century there was probably a fort there, which would
explain the tombstones of a Spanish cavalryman and another two soldiers
from the Twentieth Legion. Army veterans may have retired to Bath, but
some of the military tombstones that postdate the fort are of young men who
possibly died from illnesses they were seeking to cure there – men such as
Julius Vitalis, who had been recruited in Belgic Gaul, or Murrius Modestus,
from Forum Julii in southern France. A mason called Priscus set up an altar
at Bath – he came from the vicinity of modern Chartres. Other foreign
visitors include Rusonia Aventina, a lady of the Mediomatrices tribe (from
the area round Metz now in Germany) and Peregrinus, from near Trier.

DISEASE

Not all the introductions from the Continent were beneficial. Among the
less welcome visitors to Britain were new diseases, among them probably
leprosy. The earliest recorded case in Britain was found in the Roman
cemetery at Poundbury in Dorset, and the illness (which is first recorded in

Fig. 10. Altar from Bath, with inscription of Priscus, the stonemason from France.

India around 1400 BC) was probably spread by the Roman army. It became increasingly common until the fourteenth century, when it declined with the increase of tuberculosis.

There is also evidence for plagues in Roman Britain; there was, for example, a major European plague in AD 166–7, which is likely to have afflicted Britain, and another that recurred between 251 and 271. It has also been suggested that plague may have been a factor in the end of some towns in Roman Britain, and evidence for it has been claimed at Cirencester, Wroxeter, and Caerwent. In the case of Cirencester the evidence took the form of otherwise unexplained unburied bodies in a street ditch.

LANGUAGE

Inscriptions also provide insights into the extent and purity of Latin in Britain.

It is generally reckoned that Latin was spoken as the official language of Roman Britain, but that Celtic was still used by the majority of the uneducated. This is partly suggested by the fact that Latin did not survive and was therefore perhaps not the first language of the majority.

Many words were borrowed from Latin to become a part of the vocabulary of Roman Britain, and these survived in the post-Roman Celtic languages and are recognizable in modern Welsh. Many of the words thus borrowed were terms derived from Roman civilization, for which there were no Celtic equivalents, such as *papyrus* (paper, modern Welsh, *papyr*), *liber* (book, modern Welsh, *llyfr*), *fenestra* (window, modern Welsh *ffenestr*), *cena* (dinner, modern Welsh, *cinio*).

Words came from Christianity, and some may have been acquired in the fifth or sixth century, when Latin was still the spoken language of the Church. Words such as *pontem* (bridge) for which the Celts had a perfectly good equivalent (*briva*) may have been used to indicate that Roman bridges were greater engineering feats than Celtic ones. But why should the Roman *piscis* (fish) drive out the Celtic word, which was probably *ēscos*? This may relate to the fact that the Celts probably had no fishmongers, whereas the Romans definitely did.

The evidence for survivals into English has been debated at length, but there is no doubt that some Latin words found their way into the present-day language through Anglo-Saxon. Butter, wine, pound, inch, and mile are good examples.

Literacy was fairly widespread in the Roman period, and permeated to quite a humble level. It was noted in Chapter 2 that inscriptions in the Latin alphabet were used on the later coins of the Iron Age Celts, and this, along with the graffiti from Colchester, implies that traders at least had the rudiments of the language. The situation prevailed in the Roman period, when graffiti are found among the artisans. One inscribed a piece of pottery with the word 'SATIS' ('Enough!') and another inscribed an acid comment about a fellow worker 'Austalis has been wandering about by himself every day for a fortnight'. This, and inscriptions such as 'Verecunda the actress: Lucius the gladiator', arguably commemorating a liaison between two slaves, show just how far literacy penetrated, as does a tile from Dover with a scrawled inscription 'I made 550 box tiles' to which a wit has added 'I smashed 51'. Literacy clearly stretched to a reading of the classics, since a tag from Virgil appears on a potsherd from Silchester, while other tags from Virgil's *Aeneid* also appear on a mosaic from Lullingstone in Kent and a coin issued by the usurper Carausius.

The huge archive of documents unearthed at Vindolanda (Chesterholm), just south of Hadrian's Wall, demonstrates a high degree of literacy among Roman soldiers and their families in the early second century AD. There are now more documents surviving in the waterlogged conditions at Vindolanda than anywhere else in the Roman Empire except possibly Egypt. In the case of Vindolanda these are thin leaves of wood, with ink inscriptions, which include the only known example of shorthand and the only known example of female handwriting from the Classical world. They range from personal letters, through documents relating to the business of the fort, to an exercise done perhaps by the commandant's son which involved the copying of a comparatively obscure text from the *Aeneid*. It would seem that Claudia Severa, the commandant's wife, dictated letters (to her friend Lepidinia) to a scribe, presumably a slave, though added in her own hand the opening and flowery concluding greeting ('Farewell, sister, my dearest soul, as I hope to prosper, and hail'). The commandant, Cerialis, wrote in his own hand, in a literary and elegant Latin which seems perhaps a little forced due, it has been suggested, to his origins in Batavia on the Rhine/Scheldt. Not all the Latin is formal, and the documents show a familiarity with colloquial speech. All in all, the documentation from Vindolanda shows that the writing of good Latin was common among the officers, their wives, and slaves in northern Britain, and extended to the non-officer class and even traders. It probably did not reach at this period the people discourteously described in the Vindolanda documents as *Britunculi*, 'little Brits'.

Soon after the Conquest, so Juvenal and Martial relate, Britons were avid for instruction in rhetoric. Plutarch tells how, in AD 83, he had met at Delphi in Greece a certain Demetrius who had been sent on an official mission to some remote British islands, where he encountered a community of 'holy men' who told him their theories about meteorology and mythology. Two bronze tablets, found in York, are inscribed in Greek, perhaps by the same Demetrius giving thanks for a safe return from his voyage to distant parts.

TRADE

Britain's trade with the Continent in the Roman period was vigorous – far in excess of the pre-conquest level. In the early years, lack of manufacturing expertise meant the imports were more numerous, but as time progressed local production of Roman goods got under way. There was certainly some heavy investment in Britain just after the conquest – Seneca, Nero's minister, had staked 10,000,000 sesterces on a loan in Britain, and other Romans had similarly seen Britain as a means of getting rich quick.

The country's metal resources were the property of the State, and profit from them rapidly drained back to Rome. It is fairly clear that this source of revenue was being exploited within a few years of the conquest. The Mendips were being mined for lead which seems to have been shipped to the Continent from Bitterne, now part of Southampton. The date AD 49 appears on two frequently cited pigs (ingots) found in Britain from Mendip mines, while a British pig with the stamp of Nero has been found at St-Valery-sur-Somme. As the Roman Conquest spread, first Clwyd, then Derbyshire and Yorkshire were mined for lead. The leadworking was the responsibility of lessees, usually businessmen or freed slaves of the emperor, who worked in companies or sometimes singly. Mining rights were leased out to contractors who were closely supervised. Silver was obtained from lead, but the British sources of ore were probably of much lower grade than originally expected, and production probably lessened in the third and fourth centuries.

By the later first century AD a considerable volume of luxury goods came into Roman Britain: works of art, brooches, metal vessels, glass, and pottery. The definitive type of Roman tableware, for example (the red gloss pottery known as 'samian' or '*terra sigillata*'), was imported. Before the conquest, some had been brought in from the area around Arezzo in northern Italy, but by the time of the conquest the main centre of production had moved to southern Gaul, where factories at La Graufesenque, Montans, and Banassac, among other places, were in full production. The best was decorated with a great diversity of moulded ornament, including figures from mythology. By the early years of the second century, south Gaulish samian had been ousted by central Gaulish from Lezoux and Les Martres-

Fig. 11. 'Samian' bowl, south Gaulish, first century AD, Richborough, Kent.

des-Veyre in the Puy-de-Dome. This started to come into Britain around the turn of the first century; by the second decade of the century it had ousted the south Gaulish. A third area of production, in eastern Gaul, centred on Rheinzabern and exported some pottery to Britain in the second century. An attempt at producing homemade samian was made at Colchester in the second century, but the products enjoyed a very limited distribution. After the mid-third century, samian was not imported, but old vessels were still treasured and repaired. Such was the volume of trade that most excavated Roman sites have produced some sherds of 'samian' – it has been found even on relatively humble rural farmsteads.

Other imports included hand-mills made of Andernach lava from the Middle Rhine, and glass from Alexandria and Syria, later from the Rhineland. Small bronzes were imported from Gaul.

A large number of brooches was imported, especially in the first century AD. They include 'Aucissa' brooches, named after the Gaulish maker who put his name on them. 'Nauheim derivative brooches' and later 'knee' brooches came from Germany.

Some furniture was imported – for example, a table-leg of marble from Paros in Greece was found at Colchester. Lamps of terracotta were

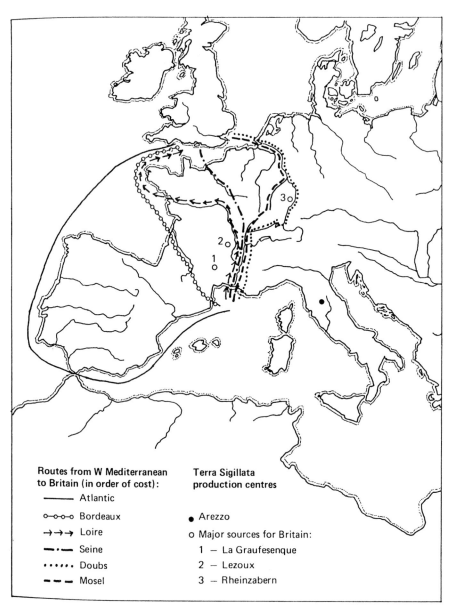

Map 4. *Transport from the western Mediterranean to Britain in the Roman period. (Source: K. Greene,* The Archaeology of the Roman Economy *(London, Batsford), p.41.)*

brought in, such as those stamped by Caius Oppius Restitutus, who worked in Italy in the late first century. Most lamps came from Gaul, what is now Germany, Africa, and Italy. The oil (olive) came from Gaul, Spain, or Africa.

Other types of pottery imports included lid-seated jars from the Eiffel-Rhine, mortaria for preparing food and vessels from Pas-de-Calais and Picardy. Rhenish ware, imitating metalwork, came from the Rhineland.

A patera (bronze saucepan) stamped by Lucius Ansius matches others from Pompeii.

The array of luxury imports to Roman Britain is impressive. There are, for example, some outstanding hoards of precious metal, such as the early fifth-century Hoxne Treasure from Suffolk, with its 14,780 coins and around 200 gold and silver objects, which include pepperpots for the spice imported from the East since the first century. Some of the plate in these hoards may have been produced in Britain, but much was clearly brought in from Gaul or further afield. The Mildenhall Treasure of silver plate, from Suffolk, was deposited around AD 360 and there are hints that it may have belonged to Eutherius, one of the highest ranking officials in the court of the emperor Julian. He may have given it as a gift to one of his British supporters. From Germany came delicate glassware, such as that from Colliton Park near Dorchester, Dorset, or that from Wint Hill in Somerset, with their engraved scenes. Other commodities imported from far afield include such objects as the gold plate with magical gnostic inscription from Caernarvon, Gwynedd. Textiles came from the Mediterranean.

Inscriptions show that commodities involved in trade included salt, pottery, wine, and fish sauce. Salt probably went across to Gaul from eastern England, along with the fine colour-coated 'castor ware' produced in the Nene valley, which turns up in the Rhineland. Many Continental merchants were involved in this cross-Channel trade, including men from Trier, Lyons, and from the lands of the Sequani in southern Gaul.

The wine trade which had begun in the Iron Age continued during the centuries of Roman rule. The main sources of information are the amphorae in which it travelled – tall storage vessels, with twin handles and pointed bases for storage in hollows in the ground. Before the conquest the main source of wine was Italy, but in the first and second centuries AD Spanish wine seems to have been imported in quantity (although some of the Spanish amphorae may have contained other perishables, such as olive oil or fish sauce).

At the end of the second century the trade in wine was disrupted due to civil war between the emperor Septimius Severus and a British usurper, Clodius Albinus. Spanish wine was one of the casualties of this exchange, but other suppliers stepped in to meet the demand, and thenceforth German wine from the Rhine and French wine from the Gironde flooded the market. An inscription of L Solimarius Secundinus of Bordeaux notes that he was a merchant involved in British trade, probably a supplier of wine, who had originated in the Rhineland. Barrels re-used as well linings at Silchester, Hants, were made of silver fir, a type of tree found no nearer to Britain than southern France. Another barrel from London was made from wood grown in the Alps.

In 276, the Emperor Probus lifted the limitations on the production of wine in France and Britain. This probably resulted in the increase of Moselle wines shipped to Britain; of British wine little is known, although vineyards have been identified at Gloucester.

British beer must always have been a popular drink, and it is mentioned in the *De Maximis Pretiis* Edict of the Emperor Diocletian at the beginning of the fourth century (an act which regulated prices in the empire). Here it was priced at twice that of Egyptian beer.

As in medieval times, wool was an important product, and mention has already been made of the *byrrus Britannicus*. Apart from this, the *De Maximis Pretiis* edict also documents the *tapete Britannicum*, a kind of woollen rug also exported from Britain. Prior to this, a garment of uncertain type called a *tossia Britannica* is mentioned in an inscription as having been sent by a governor of Britannia Inferior to a recipient in Gaul.

All this trade naturally attracted Roman traders from abroad, as inscriptions show. A certain Salmanes, who probably came from Syria, died at Auchendavy on the Antonine Wall. There is a considerable body of epigraphic evidence for trade between Britain and Gaul in the early third century. Links with Aquitaine are particularly apparent. At Bordeaux an altar was set up by Marcus Aurelius Lunaris in 237, in honour of the local goddess, and on it he is described as a merchant of both Lincoln and York; he is likely to have had commercial interests in southern Britain as well. A certain Verecundius Diogenes from Aquitaine seems to have had business interests in York, apparently supplying ships to other merchants. A Rouen trader called L Viducius Placidus operated by way of the Seine and Rhine estuaries, and traded as far afield as York. A collection of altars from Colijnsplaat (on an island in the Rhine estuary) was set up by merchants plying their trade across the North Sea in the late second and third centuries.

COINAGE

Trade in the Roman period depended on coinage. Although some Celtic coins seem to have survived in circulation to turn up associated with Roman coins in hoards, the bulk of the coinage used in Britain throughout the Roman period was imported, a common currency being in operation throughout the Roman world. In the early days following the conquest there was a shortage of bronze coins, so native imitations were produced, as they were again, in even greater numbers, in the third and fourth centuries. Some coins issued by Antoninus Pius with Britannia as a reverse design were probably struck in Britain, perhaps by a travelling mint (they are common in Britain but rare elsewhere). Apart from this, there was no official mint in Britain until the late third century usurpers Carausius and Allectus struck coins at London, Colchester, and probably elsewhere. A mint operated in London at times during the fourth century, but the main suppliers of coin were, in the early empire Rome, and in the third and fourth centuries the mints at Trier, Lyons, and Arles. Coins initially entered Britain in the army pay chests, and spread out from the forts.

Roman coins had a political as well as an economic function – they made the portrait of the emperor widely familiar, and they also communicated important messages about wars, victories, peace and even public games. Events in Britain were sometimes depicted on coins – in particular, the Claudian Conquest was commemorated (even on coins struck in the East), as was Hadrian's visit to Britain with the building of Hadrian's Wall, and the various campaigns of Septimius Severus and his sons in the north.

Coins travelled far beyond the frontiers of the province, and have been found in non-Roman contexts in Scotland and Ireland.

ROMAN RELIGION

Official Roman religion was quite different from that of the British, although essentially both were based on beliefs in the importance of natural forces. Native cults were often equated with the deities of the Roman pantheon, who frequently acquired many of the trappings and sometimes even the appearance of the native deity, to satisfy all religious sensibilities. Thus was the native deity Sul, worshipped at Bath, equated with the goddess Minerva.

The evidence for Romano-British religion is not as abundant as it is elsewhere in the empire. Romano-British religion can be grouped under a number of different heads – purely Roman 'official' religion, imported eastern cults of various types, and Romano-Celtic cults, some of which were purely native, others of which were probably derived from Gallic ones.

Of the 'official' cults, emperor worship is most readily observed in the Temple of Claudius at Colchester. Sometimes altars were dedicated to the 'spirit' of the emperor.

Two major deities were often equated with Celtic British gods. These were Mars, god of war, and Mercury, the messenger. In Gaul and Britain Mercury was seen as a trader god, and was fairly popular – a shrine dedicated to him is known from Uley, Gloucestershire, for example. Virtually all the other deities worshipped in the Roman world are represented in Britain, although some seem to have been less popular than in other parts of the empire.

A few exotic Eastern cults are represented, introduced to Britain by soldiers and traders. The Egyptian deities Isis, Serapis, Harpocrates, Bes, Thoth, and Horus; the Persian Mithras, the Phrygian Cybele, and the Syrian Jupiter Dolichenus, Sol Invictus, and Astarte were all worshipped in Britain as a direct or indirect result of Roman influence.

The most enduring of the Eastern cults was Christianity, although it had to be reintroduced after lapsing at the end of the Roman period. It was probably present in Britain from the second century onwards when it was considered subversive. Under Constantine it was declared the official religion of the empire and by 314 the Council of Arles boasted at least three British bishops. By AD 429 the Faith was so strong as to boast its own British heresy – Pelagianism.

Among the remains of Romano-British Christianity can be singled out the fine hoard of silverwork from Water Newton (Hunts) with its Christian inscriptions, which appears to include the earliest liturgical chalice from the Roman Empire. A church has been excavated at Silchester in Hampshire and the Christian rooms with their wall-paintings at the Roman villa at Lullingstone in Kent, remain the only such suite of rooms known apart from one at Dura Europos in Syria. It is clear that Christianity was not totally confined either to the towns or to the rural areas.

The most distinctive cults of Roman Britain, however, represent a fusion of Roman and Celtic beliefs. Some seem to have been native, others to be derived from Gaul. Certainly Gaulish is the cult of Epona, the horse goddess who is rarely represented in Britain. Also Gaulish are the Genii Cucullati, a trio of little figures wearing the Gaulish type of hooded cloak, the *cucullus*. They are fertility and prosperity dwarfs, and were equally favoured in Germany. Other goddesses, who frequently appear in triplicate (the Tres Matres) were popular in Britain, particularly in the Cotswolds. Clay figurines of a single mother goddess nursing a baby were made in large numbers in factories in Gaul and Germany for a Celtic clientele. Venus figurines of pipeclay, frequently found in Britain, may have been regarded as Celtic fertility goddesses.

Of the purely Celtic deities, some seem to have been given Roman counterparts. Mars was an obvious equivalent for any warrior god, and was equated, for instance, with the Celtic Belatucadrus. Some Celtic deities seem to have been paired with two or more Roman equivalents – Cocidius was one such. Other purely Celtic deities who appear from time to time in Roman Britain include Sucellos, the hammer god, and Taranis, the wheel god, both of whom can be seen (unnamed) on pottery moulds from Corbridge.

There is plenty of evidence, too, that pre-Roman cult practices continued in a Romanized guise. The pre-Celtic water goddess Coventina was worshipped at Carrawburgh on Hadrian's Wall, where offerings to her were thrown down a well.

Romano-British Art

One of the most useful barometers of Romanization can be seen in the assimilation of Roman art by the Britons.

With the conquest, the patronage for native artists provided by Celtic chiefs waned – no more did they require the panoply of war, and their wives apparently wanted Roman mirrors rather than versions decorated in the Celtic manner. To what extent Roman taste was dictated by supply and demand is a moot point. Mass-produced goods are cheaper and therefore desirable for this reason alone rather than necessarily for their style. In areas of strong resistance outside the immediate sphere of Roman influence, Celtic artistic traditions continued for a while in native media – the Brigantes were still producing metalwork to Celtic design, mostly for horse harness, at the end of the first century, as such hoards as that from Melsonby, near Stanwick (Yorkshire) show. Further north still, similar metalwork was produced among the Caledonians of northern Scotland.

Elsewhere, Celtic taste was increasingly seen only on small items for personal use. Until the end of the first century AD die-stamped mounts in Celtic style were produced for boxes and other objects, in what has been known as the 'casket ornament' tradition. Some of these, such as the mount from Elmswell, in Yorkshire, show a combination of Celtic lyre scrolls in relief and an enamelled band with ivy leaves borrowed directly from Roman art. By the end of the first century AD, however, this art was all but defunct. Even so, some Celtic motifs were used on late first and second century bow brooches which were otherwise Roman, such as the fine gilt example from Aesica (Greatchesters) on Hadrian's Wall. From this period and later, too, have come a series of openwork harness mounts with confronted trumpet patterns and triskeles in Celtic style, which seem to have been made in Roman workshops. These ornaments are found throughout the empire, and although many seem to have been made in northern Britain, others are known to have been created on the Continent, showing how widespread was the taste for Celtic ornamental motifs in the Roman world.

From the second century onwards only brooches and pins seem to keep alive Celtic motifs in a non-perishable form within the confines of

Britannia, although of course we cannot tell whether such motifs continued in textiles, leatherwork, woodwork, and impermanent art forms which have not survived.

With the conquest came both imported works of art and the arrival of craftsmen trained in Continental workshops. A good indication of this is the tombstone of Facilis from Colchester – the fact that he was not time-expired suggests it dates from the very first years of the Roman occupation, before the colonia was founded. It must have been carved by an army sculptor, trained in a Mediterranean or German workshop. Totally Classical too, and slightly later, dating from the Flavian period (towards the end of the first century) is a Sphinx tombstone with a portrait of the deceased between its paws, again from Colchester. Although the ultimate model was Egyptian, this is a Roman piece. Two early tombstones, one from Colchester and one from Gloucester, naming Rufus Sita and Longinus, were the memorials of auxiliaries, and while still thoroughly Classical are somewhat more rough-and-ready, as befitted the status of the deceased.

As far as imports were concerned, throughout the four centuries of Roman rule fine works were brought in from Italy and more frequently from Gaul. Consider, for instance, the attractive statuette of Venus from St Albans, probably of the second century, produced in Gaul, or the lamp stand in the form of Cupid from Cirencester, which may have been imported from Italy.

A fine array of imports can be seen in the assemblage of sculptures from the Temple of Mithras in London, which reached Britain in the second century. From the Mediterranean came busts of Mithras, Minerva, and the Egyptian god Serapis with a corn measure on his head. These were carefully buried in the fourth century, without their bodies, perhaps when Christianity was making Mithraism unpopular. Mithras slaying the bull surrounded by the signs of the zodiac figured on a large relief in Italian marble, and a small group of Bacchus and his followers may have come from the Danube provinces.

Also imported in about the second century was a bronze figure of an eagle from Silchester, which probably came from a statue of Jupiter, and the fine marble portrait busts from the villa at Lullingstone in Kent. Much of the silver represented in fourth century finds in Britain was of Continental manufacture, such as the huge silver plate known as the Corbridge lanx, a silver box from the London Temple of Mithras, and the finest pieces in the Mildenhall, Traprain, and Hoxne treasures, discussed above.

Not all works in Continental style were imported, as the early tombstones described above show. Mosaics frequently seem to have been made by immigrant artists, usually working in native British materials, but on rare occasions importing tesserae, for example to Lullingstone. Some British mosaics were from pattern books also available on the Continent, but by the fourth century local schools of mosaic work had distinctive styles and motifs, and most floors were laid by local artists who had clearly been trained in a classical tradition.

The subject matter of British mosaics is very diverse – from abstract patterns to spirited renderings of Roman mythical figures or deities. Bignor villa in Sussex has produced a naked, plump Ganymede being carried up to heaven, and Venus and Cupid depicted as gladiators, both floors laid down in the fourth century. Unlike most other areas of the Roman Empire, the mosaics in Britain are notable for their subject-matter, which eschews the bloodthirsty and favours gentle country scenes or myths. In Brading, Isle of Wight, the landowner spent a considerable sum on a fine fourth century mosaic of Orpheus and the beasts, and at around the same time a simple depiction of an astronomer (an example of the same subject-matter comes from Trier). The apsed dining room at Lullingstone boasted a wall-to-wall mosaic of the Rape of Europa complete with Zeus in the guise of a vigorous bull.

Only a few mosaics seem to show any style other than the purely Classical. Examples include the extraordinarily 'badly' drawn mosaics from Aldborough and from Rudston, Yorks, which are clearly only loosely based on pattern-book formulae. A mixture of cultures is also to be seen in the famous pediment with the Gorgon head from the temple of Sul Minerva in Bath, an ambiguous piece. In style it is likely to be Gaulish, but whether the huge pediment was imported or executed in Britain by a Gallic craftsman is not known.

A few items carry names. A skillet handle from the Isle of Ely seems to have been the work of a Bodvogenus. But was he Gaulish or British? The name is Celtic, and could be either.

The pottery known as castor ware is another good example of Romano-British style. The technique of piping relief ornament on pots in soft clay was Gaulish, as were the motifs used on these dark-slipped vessels made in the Nene valley; in their spirited freestyle treatment they are, however, Celtic, and must have been made by British craftsmen.

Jet from Whitby was fashioned into a variety of objects in Britain. Again there can be no question of their not being made in Britain, although some look so 'Continental' that suggestions have been made that they were the work of visiting craftsmen.

Several features tend to betray works produced by Britons with a strongly traditional training. They include distinctive treatment of eyes (large, oval, staring) and hair (formally patterned and often high, or with exaggeratedly high headgear). Extreme simplification is also a native trait.

LATE ROMAN BRITAIN

The pattern of trade and settlement established in Roman Britain in the second to fourth centuries was not to last. Once more challenges came from Europe – from within the empire itself and from barbarian tribes: the Angles and Saxons, and the Picts, Scots, and others less well documented from what are now Scotland and Ireland. These peoples became dominant in particular areas of Britain, eventually completely obliterating Roman Britannia and establishing their own areas. The period immediately after the Romans was probably the most formative in that what happened then laid down the foundations for the differences between what became England, Scotland, Ireland, and Wales.

Archaeologically, the threats can perhaps be seen in the last years of the second century and during the third and fourth, when some towns replaced their earth and timber defences with stone walls. The process of town fortification continued in the later third and fourth centuries, when in the latter period bastions were constructed, as at Caerwent in South Wales.

Long before this, however, Britain was seen as vulnerable to attack from overseas. The problems began in earnest in the later third century – a period of extreme unrest. A defensive scheme evolved, consisting of a line of coastal forts known as the Saxon Shore – still visible examples are at Richborough, Portchester, and Burgh Castle. In the fourth century the system of coastal forts was probably intended to protect Britain (under the control of an official known as the Count of the Saxon Shore) from incursions by Angles, Saxons, and others. Some of the garrisoning of these defences may have been carried out by units themselves of Germanic origin, as happened in other forts. At Housesteads, Northumberland, for example, a unit of Frisians (*Hnaudifridi*) used their own distinctive type of crude pottery which they also traded to neighbouring forts at Chesterholm and Birdoswald. An Alammanic chief, probably serving in the army, seems to have been instrumental in the proclamation of Constantine the Great as emperor at York in 306, while a certain Fraomar is recorded as a leader of Alammanic troops in Britain in 372, although again the unit he commanded was probably part of the regular army. Germanic spear types of the kind that occasionally occur in Anglo-Saxon cemeteries have been found in forts on Hadrian's Wall, and there are stray finds of Germanic objects from various contexts.

Meanwhile, in the north and west there were problems from other raiders and settlers. In the west the threat came from Ireland, and forts were built at Cardiff, Caernarvon, and possibly Caer Gybi on Holyhead in the fourth century, with further garrisons at Lancaster and Chester. To this period belongs the raiding of the quasi-historical figure Niall of the Nine Hostages; and, in the context of such raids, St Patrick's first career move was made for him when he was abducted from northern Britain to slavery in Ireland. Archaeologically there is little evidence for Irish settlement in western Britain before the later fifth century, but there is documentary evidence for attacks by Scots from northern Ireland and Picts from northern Scotland in raids on the northern part of Roman Britain in the fourth century, most notably in 367. The Saxons and others are recorded as attacking Roman Britain at the same time.

There was increasing devolution in the administration of later Roman Britain. What had been one province became two, Britannia Prima and Britannia Secunda, which were further subdivided. A fifth province seems to have been created in the fourth century. A few towns such as York, Chester and Cirencester probably became the administrative centres for their local regions.

Some economic decline in later Roman Britain has been argued, even though there are some contra-indications – such as the very late fourth century mosaics that were occasionally laid. Previously, the army had been a major factor in the maintenance of order, of economic buoyancy, and of security. Increasingly the troops were pulled out of Britain as they were needed nearer the heart of the Roman Empire. By 407 the last of the regular troops had gone and in 409 Britain was effectively no longer part of the Roman Empire.

With the removal of the army and its dependants, a major source of patronage was lost. Jobs, business opportunities, and investment were increasingly things of the past. With trade links, commerce, and organized industry shattered, it was impossible to retain lifestyles that depended on specialist items and skills. Literacy and learning appear to have declined rapidly – the very few inscriptions that have survived from the fifth and sixth centuries have been found outside the area settled by the Anglo-Saxons. Villas were gradually abandoned or readapted to more basic lifestyles.

Town life continued with varying success – some places had areas of dereliction, others kept up high standards of cleanliness. Although administrations may have remained, there was no new building in stone, although older buildings remained in commission and on occasion, for example at Wroxeter in Shropshire, new timber structures were put up. It is quite possible that many of the old towns remained as centres of regional British administrations, with a clearly defined hinterland, in some cases demarcated by linear earthworks. Gildas (a sixth century monk) speaks of some 28 'cities' existing in his own time, and it is surely to such administrations that he is referring.

Until the end of the fourth century, coinage continued to come into Britain, mainly in army coffers. The last regular copper issues to be imported reached Britain in 402, but by 430 coinage as a regular means of trade was extinct. Manufacturing, which had been carried out on a large scale and which had boomed in the market economy of the first to fourth centuries, was similarly reduced to a local level. Pottery production, often previously carried out on a huge scale, again initially to supply the army, was no longer economically viable given the decline of markets. Little wheel-made pottery was reaching the stalls in the early years of the fifth century, and by the end of its first quarter had effectively disappeared completely. Those people who had not begun using wooden or leather vessels made do with old, carefully treasured vessels.

The net result was that the mass of rural Britons were living on a level little different from that of the incoming Anglo-Saxons, except that many of the skills of home production had been lost during the previous centuries of craft specialization. Whereas it did not matter that most people in second-century Britain did not know how to make a pot or cast a brooch, by the fourth century it did. Roman Britain depended on Rome for its existence. Once abandoned it became open to other, totally different influences.

CHAPTER FOUR

The Making of England

Like Celt, the term Anglo-Saxon can be emotive – with connotations ranging from the earthy to the urbane, the complimentary to the abusive. In this shadowy period the language that is spoken throughout Britain today was established, and many English placenames date from the time. In the seventh century Christianity was adopted by most of the ruling Saxon kings and has continued in an unbroken tradition to influence social structure, laws, education, attitudes, and institutions to the present day. Although the pagan incomers were Anglo-Saxons, once Christianized they progressively became English. The fifth-century tribes developed until, by the eve of the Norman Conquest, they were a formidable English civilization. Charlemagne was prepared to acknowledge only the English king Offa as a European equal, calling him his 'dearest brother'.

THE EVIDENCE

The documentary sources for the fifth to seventh centuries (the pagan period, also known as the Dark Ages) are meagre and equalled for difficulty of interpretation only by the archaeological remains. A few late Roman sources cast the occasional glimmer of light on the earlier part of the fifth century, but native sources were written long after the events they describe. After the conversion to Christianity the sources become more reliable, although limited in their coverage. The period is therefore a minefield of controversies.

ANGLO-SAXON ORIGINS

Although the term 'Anglo-Saxon' is often used today to denote everything that is seen to be truly English, the Anglo-Saxons were Europeans who introduced a totally alien lifestyle to what had been Roman Britain. They

Fig. 12. Saxon urns, Continental and British. Left: Zuidlaren, Saxony. Right: Caistor, Norfolk.

were the enemies of Rome on the Continent and were very distinctive from both the Romans and the Celts.

The Anglo-Saxon migrations to Britain were part of a wider pattern of folk movements which characterizes the phase of European history known as the 'Great Migrations'. Although sharing common origins with the Celts, the tribes which occupied Scandinavia and the North German Plain had distinctive possessions and different types of settlement from their southern Celtic neighbours – they did not, for example, build and occupy hillforts. As with the Celts, it is through Classical writers that they are first encountered.

The Germani (who included Angles, Saxons, Thuringians, Franks, and Frisians) are mentioned by Caesar, are the subject of Tacitus' *Germania*, and are discussed by Ammianus Marcellinus in the fourth century AD. Since the bitter defeat of the Roman army under Varus in the German forests in AD 9, the Romans set the Imperial boundary on the Rhine, across which a two-way flow of merchandise, but little fraternizing, took place.

In very general terms, the picture given by the Venerable Bede in the eighth century is borne out by archaeology. In the areas he designated as settled by the Angles (basically north of the Thames), cemeteries of

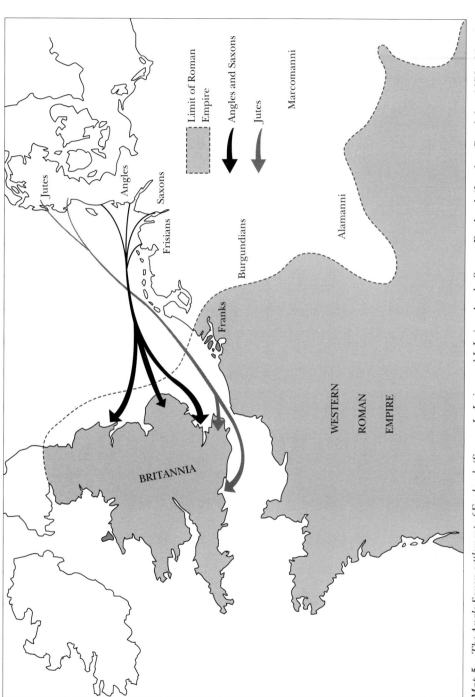

Map 5. *The Anglo-Saxon settlement of England. (Source: L. Laing and J. Laing, Anglo-Saxon England (London, Routledge, 1979), Map 1.)*

Legend:
- Limit of Roman Empire
- Angles and Saxons
- Jutes

Jutes
Angles
Saxons
Frisians
Franks
Burgundians
Marcomanni
Alamanni
BRITANNIA
WESTERN ROMAN EMPIRE

cremation burials are found, along with objects that are most readily paralleled in Anglian areas on the Continent. South of the Thames, objects show affinities to those in the Saxon areas on the Continent. In Kent and the Isle of Wight, pottery and other objects point to links with modern Jutland.

The picture is more complicated, since the sixth-century Roman historian, Procopius, refers to Frisians but ignores the Jutes, who are mentioned by Bede. The placename Swaffham, in Norfolk, probably denotes a group of Suebi, and archaeology indicates that there were also Frankish settlements south of the Thames.

Bede's description of the homeland of the Angles 'which is said from that time, to remain deserted to this day, between the territories of the Jutes and Saxons' has some corroboration in archaeology. While there are thousands of cremation burials along the Elbe and the Weser of the later fourth century, there are indeed comparatively few from the fifth, and many important sites, such as Wijister in Holland or Feddersen Wierde in Germany, seem to have been deserted around this time.

In the Elbe–Weser region rosette-stamped pots with zigzag or arched lines

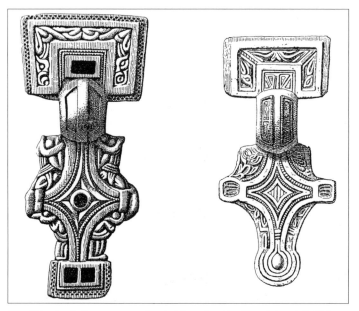

Fig. 13. Anglo-Saxon square-headed brooches, Continental and British. Left: Herpes, Charente, France. Right: Sarre, Kent. (After Salin, 1904)

Fig. 14. 'Frankish' radiate brooch, Bifrons, Kent.

have been found, and similar vessels have occurred in Norfolk at Caistor-by-Norwich and Spong Hill, from fifth century contexts. In the Caistor cemetery one pot is so close in style to a pot from Wehden in Germany, with an unusual facing human head, that it has been suggested that the pots were made by the same man who had moved both home and business.

Anglo-Saxon brooches are important evidence of settlement because they are distinctive, and their counterparts are readily datable within close brackets on the Continent. The Saxons favoured round, dish-shaped 'saucer' brooches, 'square-headed' brooches, and different types of small 'button' brooches. Among the Angles, women wore wrist-clasps, and among both Angles and Saxons, different types of 'cruciform' brooches are found, with cruciform settings of knobs on their square plate heads.

A brooch from Spong Hill with a distinctive pattern is matched on a group of brooches from Mahndorf, near Bremen, and there are other general similarities in brooch types in both areas.

Interestingly, changing Continental fashions are mirrored in England. In the fifth century and into the sixth, the dominant type of artefacts in

Kentish graves are Jutish; that is to say, their counterparts are most readily found in what is now Denmark. Gold pendants called bracteates, early forms of cruciform brooches, and distinctive square-headed brooches all echo Danish types. In the sixth century, however, growing contact with the Merovingian Franks resulted in the appearance of Frankish types of objects in graves, such as radiate-headed brooches, bird and fish brooches, and occasionally Frankish-style wheel-made pottery. In the seventh century, the grave assemblages had developed a distinctively Kentish flavour. They include composite disc brooches that are far superior to anything found among the Franks.

The tribes were barbarians – they did not live in towns, and existed in a 'heroic' rural society. They had more in common with the pre-Roman Celts than they did with Roman civilization.

Fight or Flight?

Until relatively recently this century the Anglo-Saxon presence in Britain was seen as the result of hostile invasion which caused the Romano-Britons to flee to the west. This was mostly the result of the categorical statements of Anglo-Saxon aggression in the written sources and the bitter and colourful language employed in, especially, the writing of the monk, Gildas. Inconveniently for this theory, no archaeological evidence of defences around early Anglo-Saxon settlements, no massacres, no razing, and no firing of Roman sites was forthcoming, and certainly no increase of size or number of sites in Wales. The settlements might, in theory, have been established by any number of means – threats, brute force, financial transactions, military relationships, intermarriage, or cooperation leading to dominance. More recent research supports most of these postulations to varying degrees. The best that can be said is that, like the period of the Wild West before law and order was established, the population was genuinely 'mixed' racially, socially, and culturally, and behaviour would have varied accordingly.

For a number of years recently it was argued that the Germanic settlement of England began well within the Roman period. There certainly were people of Germanic origin in the army (see p. 60) but evidence from early cemeteries shows few objects that predate *c.* AD 420. These could easily be explained as heirlooms.

The balance of the evidence now suggests that the earliest settlement proper probably took place in East Anglia; the settlement of Kent probably following very soon after. The process of immigration was probably protracted, continuing through the fifth century and into the sixth, affecting first the Upper Thames valley, the South Midlands, Surrey, Sussex, and Hampshire, then spreading to the south-east of the Humber/Severn, Yorkshire, and possibly further north.

It is interesting that Gildas (writing a sermon which attempted to explain that the ills suffered by the Britons at the time were due to their immorality) writes of a ruler, Vortigern, who emerged in the 420s and reigned for 30 years. In order to defend the territory, he settled Saxon federates (named in the *Anglo-Saxon Chronicle* as Hengist and Horsa) in the south. The way Gildas actually expressed it was, 'the ferocious Saxons (name not to be spoken!) hated by man and God, [were] let into the island like wolves into the fold' (*Gildas, The Ruin of Britain and Other Works*, tr. M. Winterbottom, London and Chichester, Phillimore, 1978).

The language he employed has not commended him to sober, dispassionate historians. Sincerity he may have had, but such emotion evokes suspicion. The incomers were, after all, pagans, and he was a monk.

A few graves of first-generation Germanic warriors do seem to corroborate these ancient opinions, notably at the Dyke Hills, Dorchester (Oxford), Richborough (Kent), and Lankills, Winchester (Hants), as well as Gloucester, Mucking in Essex, and Milton Regis (Kent). Characteristic of these burials are belt sets of types found on the frontiers of the Roman Empire in Germany (which may have been military originally but subsequently seem to have enjoyed civilian use) and a generally higher level of material equipment than might be encountered in contemporary Roman burials. Not all are male, suggesting that the 'soldiers' brought their womenfolk with them. These burials are concentrated in the extreme south of England, perhaps pointing to continuing links with late Roman Gaul and the Rhineland maintained by the Romano-British aristocracy in the early fifth century.

RELATIONSHIPS BETWEEN ANGLO-SAXONS AND BRITONS

In around 441, according to Gildas, and also found in the *Chronicle*, the Saxons rebelled and butchered a large number of the British nobility. Eventually many others migrated to Gaul. This flight is corroborated by European writers and dated by Sidonius to around 460. If the records are to be taken at face value, they would have marked a turning point in Anglo-Saxon fortunes – from then on the newcomers were the ruling élite rather than the paid help or tolerated settlers. Southern Britain was once more increasingly under European influence.

A few excavated towns have been proven to operate to the mid-fifth century, but have yielded no evidence for later occupation. These may perhaps provide supporting evidence for an exodus of the upper classes. Such depletion of the ruling class might also account for the fact that some hillforts were reoccupied in the late fifth century – that at South Cadbury, Somerset, is a dramatic example. These would now represent the new defended foci of local resistance. It is from this milieu that the most enigmatic hero of British folk-lore – King Arthur – has emanated. However, it is just as likely that the hillforts could have been fortified against other emerging Romano-British groups.

Although South Cadbury has in recent times been seen more in terms of a peaceful 'court' than a stronghold used as part of a military campaign, the fact remains that the excavated rampart and gateway were so substantial they must have been occasioned by very real fear of attack, and there are many similar, if less substantial, examples of post-Roman refortification in the west of Britain. It is possible that this might be claimed as evidence for some 'flight' westwards, but is more likely to represent a change in local living conditions.

Whether the élite fled or not, it is probable that the general pattern of settlement continued, with Anglo-Saxons taking over existing Romano-British farms and estates. A number of villa estates seem to have been utilized by people with Anglo-Saxon material possessions, though in most cases there is no evidence for the old villa buildings continuing in use. To those capable of putting up snug wooden homes there could be few attractions in the cold stone buildings which necessitated the use of boilers for the central heating and which had such unnecessary appointments as kitchens, bathrooms, and dining rooms, all requiring the ministrations of servants or slaves. Besides, stone masonry for repairs was not an Anglo-Saxon skill.

Anglo-Saxon building techniques were generally distinct from Romano-British and, therefore, when discovered are relatively easy to identify. They were practical to put up without the organization of civilization. The sunken floor hut with timber superstructure became ubiquitous in the areas of Anglo-Saxon settlement, and the typical large, rectangular timber hall, often with buttresses, is well exemplified at Chalton (Hants) or West Stow (Suffolk).

At Barton Court Farm (Oxfordshire) timber buildings were put up by the new occupants alongside the villa. At Orton Hall Farm (Northants) timber buildings were similarly erected, and associated finds included a Frisian comb. At Orton Longueville (Cambs) a farmstead was built adjacent to the villa in the fifth–sixth century, making use of one of the Roman paddocks. Charter evidence in Dorset suggests that the land boundaries followed by the Anglo-Saxons were of Roman origin, and studies of other areas, such as Humberside, seem to endorse this. In point of fact, territorial divisions, already demarcated by field boundaries, lanes, and banks, would have been difficult and certainly pointless to redivide. It is also the case that there was a pre-existing workforce tied to the old farms, and this could be pressed into labouring for the new masters, in some cases (as Gildas implies) by slavery.

However, to counterbalance this picture of Britons as second-class citizens, several of the major Anglo-Saxon leaders have British names – Cerdic, who founded Wessex, is one, and later kings include Merewalh ('famous Briton') of Mercia and Caedbaed of Lindsey. Ceawlin and Cynric had Irish–British names. Since parents do not call their children names that have negative associations for them, and people do not assume such names, the implication must be that British and Anglo-Saxon relations were not always confrontational.

Ceawlin, however, according to the *Chronicle* could be aggressive and was responsible for razing the last remaining Roman cities in 577/8 – Bath, Cirencester, and Gloucester. On what level these places operated has yet to be discovered. A few early Anglo-Saxons seem to have settled within the walls of towns, next to their British neighbours, but towns, like villas, ceased to be important factors in the landscape of Britain.

As further evidence of cooperative relationships between the two peoples, structures excavated at Cowdery's Down, Hampshire, suggest that Romano-British building techniques in timber may have influenced Anglo-Saxon styles. The general architectural model can be seen in the timber structures put up in the late Roman period at Wroxeter or in Romano-British 'barn dwellings'. Some Romano-British metalworking techniques and artistic motifs may have been taken over by the Anglo-Saxons.

The situation in Britain was in marked contrast to that which prevailed on the Continent. There the situation was reversed, in that the Frankish incomers were culturally and socially the inferiors of the people on whose land they settled, and, more strangely, seem to have acknowledged this fact. If it is possible to accept as true the exodus of the British nobility, Gaul would have been especially wealthy at this time and the British contingent perhaps now amenable to a less confrontational approach to the barbarians. In Gaul, the language of the original inhabitants survived to influence the development of that of the incomers – modern French is a Romance language, not Germanic. In Britain it has already been noted that very few Latin words survived (except later through the Church) to become a part of Anglo-Saxon speech, and even placenames became predominantly Anglo-Saxon outside the Celtic/British areas (see below).

In southern Britain the Anglo-Saxon tongue came into general use. Basic words such as house (hūs), come (cuman), foot (fōt), hand (hand), fickle (ficol), widow (widewe), wife (wīf), and hive (hȳf) are all Old English and have survived from this period.

THE FORMATION OF KINGDOMS

The early Anglo-Saxons introduced a new kind of social hierarchy in which the essence of control lay in the relationship of the leader to his war band. It is extremely likely that in the early days of the first settlements, the social groupings were small, comprising the war leader and his band of fighting men which was small enough for him to know each member individually.

The multiplicity of war leaders is probably reflected in the large number of placenames meaning 'the village of X's people' – examples are Hastings (Haestingas is recorded as the name of a tribe in Sussex), the (many) Rodings (the people of Hroda), Reading (the people of Read(a)). It is notable that this type of placename is also found in Germany – for example Sigmar*ingen* (Sigimar's people). It is now believed that these placenames probably relate to the period after the spread of Christianity rather than the immediate period of settlement when, presumably, the Romano-British names were used.

Later developments are reflected in the *-ham* and *-tun* suffixes (homestead and fence), referring to the type of habitation. Sometimes these elements are added to the *-inga* element as in Birmingham (the ham of Beornmund's people), or Whittington (tun of Hwita's people).

Some hybrid names occur that represent a mixture of Anglo-Saxon and British. These are usually names which represent Anglo-Saxon versions of old Romano-British names. Thus Gloucester comes from the Roman name, Glevum, which is in fact a Roman version of the older Celtic name meaning 'bright place', to which has been added the Anglo-Saxon word for fort, *ceaster.*

The Anglo-Saxons divided England up into shires in the ninth and tenth centuries. The word *scir,* which originally was used to describe a 'subdivision of people', later came to be used to describe a land division occupied by a group of people. Although some names for shires reflect their Celtic past, notably Cornwall and Devon (Devon means 'the deep ones' and is a translation of the Celtic tribal name, Dumnonii), most (except the now vanished Rutland, which is post-conquest) are Anglo-Saxon. Some are tribal names, such as Essex or Sussex. Others, such as Kent, are simply tribal names without a suffix. Dorset and Somerset are also tribal names, to which the Anglo-Saxon word *saete* ('settlers') has been added. Northumberland has the tribal name to which a suffix meaning 'a large tract of land' has been added.

The growing political configurations of the pagan period are probably also reflected in the regional names – Sussex, Wessex, Essex (the south, west, and east Saxons). East Anglia – the east Angles – is divided into the north people (Norfolk) and those of the south (Suffolk).

The process of state formation was fairly slow, and not until the sixth century is there any real evidence of a system of kings and over-kings and the formation of larger tribal areas. The first region in which state formation was apparent was Kent, and eventually further kingdoms were formed, including East Anglia, Northumbria, Mercia, and Wessex.

TRADE AND CONTACTS

The continuing arrival of foreign objects on British soil proves that the newcomers maintained close links with their old homelands. Pagan Saxon England has yielded a considerable diversity of imported objects, and these seem to have entered the country by way of Kent. Amethyst beads may have come from Spain or from the east Mediterranean, and finds are often associated with 'Coptic' bowls and cowrie shells. Ivory rings, of which 112 examples are known mostly from East Anglia, appear to be of elephant ivory rather than walrus (which was popular later in the Anglo-Saxon period), and must have come via the Mediterranean. Amber beads seem to have come from the Baltic, and are distributed in eastern and central England, with lesser concentrations in Kent. The largest number from any one site was nearly 1,000 from Sleaford in Lincolnshire. They seem to have come into the country from different points of entry.

Rock crystal beads could have been made from British material but are more likely to have been imported, and share a similar distribution to the amber beads and ivory rings. One of the most unusual categories of object comprises balls of rock crystal. The pieces of crystal are so large that they are most unlikely to be British (although some lumps large enough occur in Scotland), and are more likely to have come from Switzerland or Germany. Glass vessels seem to have been imported from Merovingian Gaul, which also provided wheel-made pottery and coins.

Prior to AD 625 the coins imported were gold issues, which have been found distributed mostly in Kent and the Upper Thames. It is likely that gold coins were the main source for jewellery. Although a few are Byzantine, most are Merovingian and other derivative issues. The sources for these coins were in southern France, notably Lyons, Vienne, Marseilles, and Arles.

After 625 the axis shifted, and most of the coins came from around Paris and the Meuse and Moselle regions. This shift coincided with the devaluation of gold. During the later sixth and seventh centuries balances were buried in graves, often with weights made out of Roman coins or with purpose-made weights. One was from Byzantium. Sometimes they have been found with touchstones for assaying the quality of gold. This implies that by this time there was a need to regularize trade and set particular values on gold – the coins were clearly not being used as currency. Coins were used in wergild payments (made by kin to wronged families), and were in effect special-purpose money. They were status objects, and were sometimes mounted into necklaces. Serving a similar purpose to the coins were imported gold die-stamped pendants known as bracteates, produced in Scandinavia. They have been found in Kent and East Anglia, where silver ornaments known as 'scutiform pendants' are also found.

By the middle of the seventh century growing trade between the south-east of England and Merovingian Gaul prompted the issue of Anglo-Saxon gold coins, modelled on the Continental. These *thrymsas*, as they are called, are extremely rare – they have mostly come from a single hoard found at Crondall in Oxfordshire – and are unlikely to have been used in ordinary trade. Towards the end of the century, however, they were progressively debased in line with contemporary developments on the Continent until they were essentially silver pieces. These are known as *sceattas*, and their varied designs seem to be of Anglo-Saxon inspiration and, on occasion, to have been modelled on Continental, sometimes Roman, patterns. One of the most common series is known as 'Anglo-Frisian' as it appears to have been issued for trade with the towns of Frisia.

Anglo-Saxon coinage, indeed, continued closely to follow developments in mainland Europe. In due course, when the Franks introduced the larger silver *denier*, two kings in Kent followed suit, striking similar pennies. King Offa, who took over the Kentish mint when he conquered the area in the late eighth century, continued to strike pennies for trade with the Continent. More remarkably, Offa struck a gold dinar with Arabic legends, which was probably designed for trade with the Moors in Spain.

The rich cemetery at Sutton Hoo, near Woodbridge, Suffolk, excavated in 1939 and currently once more the focus of archaeological attention, is characterized by the diversity of its burials. In the early seventh century the ruling dynasty in the area, the Wuffingas, had come from Sweden, thus representing yet another element in the immigrant population. The most famous of the Sutton Hoo burials, mound 1, is seen to have been the memorial of one of the East Anglian kings who died around the end of the first quarter of the seventh century. The tomb was a ship (a burial custom found in variant form in another mound at Sutton Hoo, and at Snape, also in Suffolk) in accordance with Swedish practice. The grave was furnished with a rich array of artefacts, many of gold and garnet. Certain objects in the burial cache, however, were either made by an immigrant Swedish craftsman, or, much more probably, were imported from Sweden. They include the king's remarkable vizor-masked helmet and his shield. The jewellery was probably made in a local workshop, under the direction of a master craftsman, but even here the influence of Sweden is apparent. The other objects in the deposit also point to far-flung contacts. Apart from a few items probably of Celtic workmanship, there was a silver dish from the Imperial Byzantine workshops at Constantinople, another silver dish of Mediterranean origin, a bronze bowl with drop handles also from the east Mediterranean, and a purse of coins from Merovingian Gaul. The gold coins are likely to have been diplomatic gifts. The east Mediterranean items were old, and were probably traded via Merovingian France, as were the garnets at Sutton Hoo and in jewellery found elsewhere in south-east England in the later sixth and seventh centuries. These garnets had probably originated in India and been traded westwards to Constantinople.

Such objects were not part of a casual trade, but high-status items used in top-level international and internal gift exchanges. As the Anglo-Saxon kings in the later sixth and seventh centuries became more powerful and ruled over larger domains, they accumulated wealth and status symbols, increasing their stature with gifts to their fellow kings. This is the explanation for the so-called 'Coptic' bowls in rich Saxon graves (long thought to have come from Egypt, but more probably Byzantine), which are found in Kent, with a scatter along the Upper Thames, East Anglia, and into Hampshire.

The distribution of imported objects of the sixth to seventh centuries in England suggests two patterns of trade, one between the Continent and Kent, and one with East Anglia. Within Kent, Sarre and Dover may have been the main points of entry. Large numbers of wheel-thrown bottles appear in the immediate hinterlands, perhaps connected with a wine trade. The counterpart of Sarre was probably Quentovic in Frisia. During the seventh century, Fordwich in Kent, Ipswich in East Anglia, and Hamwic (Southampton) in Hampshire became three of the most important trading bases.

Law codes shed some light on Anglo-Saxon overseas trade in this period. The Laws of Wihtraed set down around AD 695 decree that foreigners or travellers from afar should shout or blow a horn when leaving a road, to show they are not thieves.

Relatively few exports from Britain have been found on the Continent, but textiles are likely to have been one commodity. Braids brocaded with gold may have been exported – similar examples have been found at Chessel Down in the Isle of Wight and Herpes-en-Charente in France, a cemetery site which has also produced other types of Anglo-Saxon object.

RELIGION AND ART

The incoming Continental people were pagans until at least the seventh century. Their beliefs were enduring enough to bequeath the names for the days of the week called after deities – Wednesday (Woden), Thursday (Thunor), Friday (Frigg). Remarkably little is known about pagan Anglo-Saxon religion except by inference from the Viking Age, but the evidence from cemeteries provides pictures of belief in the afterlife and the cult practices, which included, as Sutton Hoo is currently so graphically showing, human sacrifice. Some structures, identified as shrines, have been detected in excavation.

Although drawing heavily upon late Roman decoration for its inspiration, Anglo-Saxon art was quite different from Roman. The artists favoured stylized animals and occasional human masks, broken down into component parts in all-over decoration, and later ribbon patterns of snakes. They rarely, if ever, favoured naturalistic representation – a rare exception is a clay figure of a seated man on a pot lid from Spong Hill. They did not subscribe to Classical ideas about the role of the human figure in art.

The coming of Christianity

Rome may have removed her legions, but some two centuries later she arrived once more with a subtler form of domination – religious belief. Until the time of Henry VIII the influence exerted was all-embracing. Even after Henry's break from Roman Catholicism the influence remained, if only because the English Church still operated in terms of Roman faith – reacting against it.

The spread of Christianity had an enormous impact on Anglo-Saxon society as a whole. For one thing, it forged a common religious bond with the Continent, paving the way for greater political ties and trade. For another, it linked the Anglo-Saxons to a system that was essentially Mediterranean and city-based. It provided a new set of values and a new intellectual climate in which ideas and ideologies could flourish.

In AD 597 St Augustine arrived in Kent with the express intention of introducing Christianity to the Anglo-Saxons. The foundations for the Augustinian mission had been laid in the years leading up to 597, since Ethelbert the king of Kent had married a Frankish princess, Bertha, who brought with her to Canterbury her own chaplain, Liuhard. According to Bede, Liuhard used a former Roman church (usually identified as St Martin's in Canterbury, a mostly later building which nevertheless has some Roman masonry in its structure). A hoard of ornaments found in the grounds of this church included a pendant with very Frankish-looking stone settings, but the most notable was a gold medallet bearing the name of Liuhard himself. Given the close ties between the Kentish kingdom and the Franks (who were, since the time of Clovis (481–511), professed Christians), a political objective probably lay behind the mission, since it would have been seen as strengthening ties with the Continent. In any event, Augustine came with a procession of clerics in Roman vestments, bearing books and holy objects to awe the pagan Saxons, and began the process of conversion with the Kentish royal family.

In his account, Bede makes the point that the missionaries built their new churches in stone. It was an assertion of the Roman origins of the new faith, and the new churches were designed to basilican plans formulated in the Mediterranean. The first church to be built was that of St Augustine himself, constructed at Canterbury and dedicated to SS Peter and Paul. As burials were not permitted in the body of the church, it was flanked by side chapels called *porticus* which contained the graves of the royal family of Kent, Liuhard, St Augustine, and his successors. Roman bricks were used in the fabric, as they were in nearby St Mary's.

A series of these missionary churches was built in the seventh century in Kent, of which perhaps the finest was Reculver. This survived until the nineteenth century when it was reduced to foundations on the whim of the vicar's mother. An outlier in Essex was St Peter's, Bradwell-on-Sea, which was built by St Chad in the remains of a Saxon Shore fort and still stands more or less intact.

The spread of Christianity was slow, since conversion was effected at the top and the mass of the populace was much less prepared to abandon the old faiths. St Paulinus took the Faith to Northumbria, where he preached to the assembled followers of Edwin at Yeavering (the grandstand at which he probably did this was found by archaeologists). At Yeavering, alongside the palaces of the Northumbrian kings, have been found a timber chapel and Christian graveyard, as well as evidence for earlier pagan practice.

The process of conversion was also uneven. In East Anglia an early success was followed by a lapse into paganism, and in Mercia the powerful king, Penda, opposed the new faith almost as vigorously as he conducted his military campaigns.

Christianity brought books, art, and learning to Britain from the Continent. Among the books that Augustine himself brought was a Gospel (alas badly damaged by a fire in the eighteenth century), produced in Italy. We are told that in Northumbria the patron of the monasteries of Monkwearmouth and Jarrow – Benedict Biscop – made journeys to Rome and brought back relics, books, and icons. Ceolfrith, abbot of Jarrow, also built up a major library which was subsequently drawn upon by Bede.

CHRISTIAN SAXON ART AND CONTINENTAL CONTACTS

The art introduced through Christianity was at considerable variance with that of the pagan Anglo-Saxons, but it was not long before the Anglo-Saxon artists (and the Celtic in their own lands) grafted ornament from their own repertoire on to the naturalistic traditions of the Mediterranean. The Insular Gospel Books such as the Book of Durrow or Lindisfarne Gospels show just how successful they were in combining quite disparate traditions in a seamless fusion.

The eighth century was a period of growing cultural interplay between England and the Continent. Once converted, the Anglo-Saxons rapidly began to carry the Christian flag to pagan areas on the Continent. Frisia was an area targeted by Northumbrian monks; the first mission was that of St Wilfrid who was joined in 718 by St Boniface, who extended the missionary work to Thuringia and Hesse.

Archbishop Theodore and Abbot Adrian came to Canterbury from the Mediterranean, and there established a famous school of learning. From Canterbury scholars went forth to other parts of England. Among them was Aldhelm who had additionally benefited from study under Irish clerics at Malmesbury. Aldhelm's influence extended to other centres in Wessex.

To further the building of the new church at Jarrow, masons were brought from Gaul, where the neat coursing of the walling in the still partly surviving building perhaps attests their skill. Recent work suggests that the whole of the grandiose building scheme to be seen in Northumbria was the direct outcome of Frankish inspiration, seen in the monasteries at Vienne, St Etienne in Paris, Jouarre, and elsewhere, and that Frankish influence, too, may have been behind the introduction of stained glass at Monkwearmouth and Jarrow. The appearance of Mediterranean-style sculpture may also reflect Frankish influence, if not Italian. Inhabited vinescroll – vine tendrils with birds and beasts eating the fruit – was a Mediterranean device that subsequently appeared on Northumbrian crosses, such as that at Ruthwell, Dumfriesshire, while the draperies of the figures on both the Ruthwell and Bewcastle crosses betray an awareness of Mediterranean models.

Northumbria long remained pre-eminent in English learning. A school was set up at York under Egberht, Bede's pupil, and students came from the Continent as well as from many part of England. The most celebrated of the pupils at York was Alcuin, who was responsible for coordinating the Gallic revival of learning under Charlemagne, the Carolingian renaissance, as it has been called. Prior to the Carolingian period Frankish art had not been very distinguished, but through the inspiration of Anglo-Saxon and

Celtic models there grew up what has been termed the Ada School of Carolingian art in the years following 780. Meanwhile, missionary work continued on the Continent under such Anglo-Saxon monks as Willehad and Aluberht, and the Insular style was transmitted, along with manuscripts, to Continental monasteries.

URBAN REVIVAL

Although there was apparently no continuity between the old Romano-British towns and their Anglo-Saxon replacements in terms of trade (despite some lingering occupation inside town walls), towns did become an important feature of Anglo-Saxon life. They were a direct response to growing Continental links. Eventually, whether they had been totally abandoned or not, many Roman foundations were revived. However, the earliest Saxon towns were not like their walled Roman predecessors, but were open, undefended trading bases located near the coast and linked to inland religious and royal seats. These early English towns were the counterparts of such North Sea coastal trading bases as Dorestad and Quentovic in Frisia, the administrative and ecclesiastical centres (London and York, for example) being perhaps the equivalents of Cologne.

The most extensively excavated trading base is Hamwic (Southampton), which was abandoned in the Middle Ages in favour of a site to the south-east, and not built up again until Victorian times. Its 30 ha were laid out with gravelled streets lined with houses with industrial areas to their rear. Coins were struck for overseas trade, which certainly extended to Frisia (attested by coins, bone combs, and a distinctive flute), as well as to Frankish Gaul (attested by pottery and other objects). Glass was imported from the Rhineland and probably from the East, by way of Continental markets. Pottery came from the Meuse, Pas-de-Calais, and the Ardennes, as well as from Trier in Germany and Rouen in France. Huge querns for grinding grain were imported from the Niedermendig lava quarries. Even more far-flung trade was indicated by the bone of a green turtle, now found no nearer than the Canary Islands.

Hamwic and its counterparts, such as Fordwich in Kent or Ipswich in Suffolk, were not defended, although defensive works were a feature of the development of towns (burhs) in Mercia in the late eighth and early ninth centuries. These towns were planned with a regular layout, and represent the first step towards true urbanism in England, though their original *raison d'être* was probably defence against the Vikings. Many are built on Roman sites, others have manorial origins, and the majority still flourish today – Stafford, Tamworth, and Hereford for example. They were probably developed *c.* 780–90 by Offa, a king whose ties with the Continent were strong and who was regarded with respect by Pope Adrian. A marriage alliance between Charlemagne's son and Offa's daughter was proposed, but Offa's demand of a corresponding marriage between his son and Charlemagne's daughter led to a three-year dispute in which all English ports were closed to Frankish trade.

THE LATE SAXONS

The links with Carolingian Europe forged by Offa were consolidated during the later ninth and tenth centuries. Anglo-Saxon art had long been subject to other influences – Pictish, Irish, Germanic, even Byzantine – and the borrowing went both ways. So intertwined were the traditions that it is not always easy to determine whether a book was produced in England or on the Continent. The Maaseik Gospel may have been produced in York or at Echternach: scholars cannot agree. The Trier Gospels was the work of two monks, one with English handwriting and an English name 'Thomas', the other with French-style lettering. The page of Canon Tables in the book, however, executed by the English monk, copies an Italian model. Flourishing in the north of France in Carolingian times was a tradition called Franco-Saxon, ultimately derived from a Northumbrian background. From the same background came another tradition in Bavaria and western Austria, well exemplified by the Cutbercht Gospels, which also displays Italian influence. It is apparent from the *Liber Pontificalis* (the Book of Popes) that Anglo-Saxon craftsmen were so highly regarded in Rome they were allowed to make plate for the altar of St Peter. Many major pieces of Continental ornamental metalwork betray Anglo-Saxon ornamental influence if not manufacture – works such as the Tassilo Chalice from Austria or the Rupertus Cross from Salzburg.

Carolingian influence is apparent in several spheres of English life, but nowhere is it more apparent than in art. A Carolingian feature that gained widespread acceptance in England was acanthus foliage ornament – acanthus is a broad-leaved Mediterranean plant. Perhaps its earliest manifestation is on the gold and enamelled head for a reading pointer known as the Alfred Jewel. An inscription round its edge implies that it was made on the orders of King Alfred himself. The finest manifestation of acanthus, however, is on the embroideries executed in Wessex for the Shrine of St Cuthbert at Chester-le-Street in Co. Durham. Inscriptions show that they were produced on the orders of Queen Aelfflaed for the bishop of Winchester, and indicate that they were woven between 909 and 916. Despite the acanthus, they are without any obvious parallel in the Carolingian world, and mark the beginning of the outstanding phase of late Saxon art known as the Winchester School. This tradition stemmed from monastic reforms which were, in turn, inspired by similar reforms on the Continent.

From the outset Winchester art shows a strong debt to Carolingian. It is apparent, for example, in what is arguably the finest of the Winchester manuscripts, the Benedictional of St Aethelwold. Produced between 963 and 985, it displays miniatures modelled on Carolingian ivories produced at Metz, and uses a type of Carolingian lettering which remained popular thereafter.

Late Saxon churches, too, often reflect Continental trends, for example it has been suggested that Carolingian and Ottonian architecture was the inspiration behind the arcading that appears on the towers at Earl's Barton (Northants) and Barton-on-Humber (Lincs); Continental influence may also be behind the elaborate westworks and crossings found in some churches. Saxon church architecture is distinctive – windows have jambs and lintels made from one massive stone, arches are high (they can be three times as high as they are wide) and round-headed, based on Roman models. The chancel arches at Escomb and Corbridge may even have been re-used from nearby forts.

Late Saxon England was culturally far removed from that of the sixth century. In many respects it led Europe in its art, learning, and institutions – towns in Anglo-Saxon England in particular were a model for the Continent.

LATE SAXON TOWNS

In Wessex, Alfred the Great (AD 871–99) was responsible for the foundation of a number of *burhs*, which served the double function of fortifications and places of refuge in the face of Danish attacks, and as mercantile centres. These towns were laid out with grid-iron street plans, had earth-and-timber defences, and streets devoted to particular industries. Some were established where there was a concentration of settlement, for example Malmesbury or Shaftesbury. Where there were existing Roman towns, the Roman walls dictated the layout, but where the towns were founded on new sites, they were laid out on a rectilinear plan. The new street plans did not follow the Roman, except where the existence of Roman gates dictated the arterial thoroughfares. The assumption must be that the Roman streets and buildings had virtually disappeared – but the inspiration was probably Roman town planning. *Burhs* were established around 20 miles apart, and each had a mint and market. They were the most sophisticated towns of ninth-century Europe (although there was an expansion of Carolingian town building at the same time), and the process of town development was extended into Mercia by Aethelflaeda, Alfred's daughter. Each town had to put a number of men into the battlefield when the occasion arose, the number of men being dictated by the number of hides of land the town comprised – lists were kept by Alfred's son Edward the Elder in a document called the *Burghal Hidage*. Once established, the towns enabled further interchange with Europe.

LATE SAXON TRADE

Through the towns, late Saxon England enjoyed a vigorous trade with the Continent. The Saxon writer Aelfric in his *Colloquy* described a merchant as saying, 'I go on board my ship with my freight and row over the regions of the sea, and sell my goods and buy precious things which are not produced in this land, and I bring it hither to you with great danger over the sea, and sometimes I suffer shipwreck with the loss of all my goods, barely escaping with my life' (tr. D. Whitelock, *The Beginnings of English Society*, Harmondsworth, Pelican, 1952, p. 125).

Aelfric also relates how the goods he brought back were 'purple robes and silk, precious gems and gold, rare garments and spices, wine and oil, ivory and brass, copper and tin, sulphur and glass and many suchlike things'.

Near Eastern glass has been found at places as far apart as London, Chichester, and Yorkshire. Schist whetstones came from the Eiffel, pottery came from the Rhineland and France. Much of the trade was in the hands of foreign merchants, particularly Frisians, though traders from Rouen, Flanders, Ponthieu, Normandy, Huy, Liège, Nivelles, and the Holy Roman Empire were all documented in London around AD 1000. Laws controlled foreign trade and merchants. Cnut (1016–35) negotiated protection for his merchants on foreign soil, as well as freedom from certain dues, and Aelfric mentions English traders in Rome, a fact perhaps supported by the discovery of English coins there. Sometimes foreign ships had to obtain licences to enter a port – if this were not done, cargoes could be confiscated and seamen fined. A law code of *c.* 1000 allowed foreign merchants in London to buy wool, fat, and three live pigs for their ships, but the wool had to be bought after unloading, instead of direct from the ship in harbour. Among documented imports to London around this time were fish, wine, and blubberfish – wine was imported in particular from Rouen. Slaves, too, were a commodity of trade – these were exported from Bristol as late as the eleventh century.

Ships were specially built to handle the cross-Channel trade, and one such, still containing pottery sherds of French or Belgian origin and datable to the tenth century, was found at Graveney in Essex.

The English, as they now were, are also attested abroad – an English merchant called Botta was recorded as operating in Marseilles in the eighth century.

Various categories of imported wares have been recognized in England. From the Rhineland came Badorf ware – large amphorae or storage jars decorated with rouletted strips, which must have arrived filled with wine or other perishable materials, from the eighth century onwards. Pingsdorf ware was another Rhineland import. Made of pimply ware with splashes of dark red paint, it came made in a variety of forms and reached many parts of England. The area from which red-painted ware was purchased later became Normandy, and the pottery was traded after the Norman

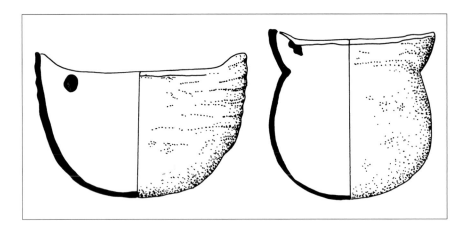

Fig. 15. 'Frisian' bar-lug pots, British and Continental (restored). Left: Barking, Essex. Right: Leeuwarden, Holland.

Conquest. Other types of imports included Tating ware, from the Low Countries, decorated with lozenges of tinfoil, and bar-lug cooking pots, which made an impact on the local pottery tradition of Cornwall – it may have been introduced by a group of immigrants from Frisia.

Among the other categories of import in later Saxon England were whetstones of schist from the Eiffel, and querns made from stone quarried at Niedermendig and Mayen.

THE CELTIC WEST

During the period of the Anglo-Saxon settlements, the Irish Sea served as an important route for the migration of people, artefacts, and ideas around the 'Celtic Mediterranean'. It also served as a routeway for the flow of trade and ideas from Europe, and, more particularly, the Mediterranean.

The western and northern Celts had never been Romanized, but from the second century AD onwards a series of factors, internal and external, led to new political groupings being formed and the gradual development of kingdoms that crystallized in the fifth and sixth centuries AD. Roman influence may have played some part in Scotland and Wales, but from the fifth century onwards there was a growing interplay between the Celts and the Mediterranean world.

Christianity took root on Celtic soil before it did in Anglo-Saxon areas. There may have been some Christian communities established in the hinterland of Hadrian's Wall and in and around the south Welsh towns of Caerwent and, less certainly, Carmarthen. In addition, Christianity probably flourished in some of the north Welsh and Cumbrian forts. It also seems likely that a Christian community was established at Whithorn in Galloway sometime around the late fourth or early fifth century. Certainly, by the late fifth century memorial stones in Galloway, Cornwall, and Wales show that in these areas Christianity had already become well established. In Ireland Christianity was established by Patrick and Palladius around the beginning of the fifth century. Northern Scotland was converted rather later, beginning with the activities of St Columba, the Irish monk who founded a monastery at Iona in 567, from where the slow process of the conversion of the Picts was carried out.

Although the roots of this Celtic Christianity lay in the Roman period, it seems likely that it was reinforced by contact with Europe. The evidence for this takes the form of imported pottery from the east Mediterranean. This seems to have arrived in the late fifth and sixth centuries. It comprises amphorae (wine storage vessels) from the Aegean, probably the Greek Argolid and from Cilicia and Antioch in Syria. Alongside these are found olive-oil amphorae from Tunisia, jars from Sardis in Turkey, African red-slipped dishes from Tunisia, and others from western Turkey. The British assemblages of finds differ markedly from those from south-west Europe, implying that trade came directly from the East. The likeliest origin for the trade lies in the Byzantine world itself, the commodity sought in exchange probably being tin.

A tombstone at Penmachno, Gwynedd, proclaims that it was set up '*in tempore Justinis consulis*' – the consul Justinus was in office in AD 540, but had no jurisdiction outside the Mediterranean. Other tombstones use formulae which show direct Christian influence from North Africa and southern Gaul.

A second pattern of Celtic trading was directly with Gaul. It is distinguishable again in the sixth and seventh centuries by a trade in pottery, probably from the Bordeaux region, possibly accompanying a trade in Gaulish wine for which archaeological evidence does not exist but for which there is some documentary support.

IRELAND AND THE CONTINENT

There is considerable evidence for Irish missionary activity on the Continent, with monasteries being founded there by Irish monks. In the fifth century the Atlantic ports were the centre of a pattern of trade which extended from Iberia through the Irish Sea to north-west Scotland. Throughout this arena the cult of St Martin was disseminated, probably as a secondary result of the trade.

It was to the model of St Martin, who founded a monastery at Tours, that the early Irish Church looked in designing its monasteries. The rectilinear planning of such early foundations as Clonmacnois and Iona was due to inspiration which came ultimately from the east Mediterranean. Columba's biographer, Adomnan, reported that Gaulish sailors regularly visited Iona, while a *Life of St Cybard* said of Bordeaux that 'ships from Britain equipped with sail and oar arrive at the port of the city to do trade there'.

From the sixth century Irish monks were travelling to Italy and Gaul, and, slightly later, to Germany, while some Continental monks came to Ireland to study. Columbanus set up a hermitage on the Vosges at Annegray; other Irish monasteries were founded at Luxeuil, St Gall, and Bobbio. In Italy, Irish monks learned Italian scripts but developed their own ornamental devices, which were taken back to Ireland to fuel the development of Insular manuscript art. At Bobbio manuscripts in the library included some from North Africa.

From Spain, Ireland acquired the writings of Isidore of Seville, possibly by an indirect route from Bobbio; Isidore, like the Irish monks, was interested in Hebrew, Greek, and Latin. Pagan classical texts as well as Christian were studied in Irish monasteries – a seventh-century commentary on the *Bucolics* and *Georgics* of Virgil was available in early medieval Ireland.

The Celtic art that developed in Britain and Ireland is a good example of how many stimuli contributed to the development of an Insular tradition. Current thinking supports the view that a survival of Romano-British ornament in fifth and sixth century Britain provided the genesis of the style, which was transmitted to Ireland. The sudden flowering of Irish art, however, probably came about in the later seventh century through the influence of Iona, which was the recipient of ideas from Anglo-Saxon England, from the neighbouring Picts, and from the Continent. The library at Iona contained books from many parts of Europe and further afield, and ideas were drawn from them in the development of a sophisticated Christian iconography, well displayed in the *Book of Kells*.

It was into this world, and that of the early English kingdoms, that the Vikings intruded in the late eighth and ninth centuries AD.

CHAPTER FIVE

The Vikings

Gentle farmers or savage seafarers? The Vikings as part of European legend were fierce warriors who terrorized Europe from their northern homelands – fearless brigands intent on loot, pillage, rape, and murder. Although there is no evidence that Viking raiders ever wore such headgear, as a result of Hollywood films, the horned helmet has become the symbol of the Viking – a kind of visual shorthand that instantly conveys a set of concepts that need no further explanation. Yet, on balance, the concrete evidence shows a different picture.

Most of the modern myth of the Vikings is attributable to ancient sources. The earliest targets for Viking raids were frequently monasteries and churches, which offered rich, easy pickings. Sadly for Viking public relations, the chief chroniclers of contemporary events were men of the Church. For them the Viking raiders comprised a double outrage – they were not only pagans, but they chose to loot God's churches.

The English monk Alcuin wrote of the raiders: 'We and our forefathers have lived here for about 350 years, and never have such terrors as these appeared in Britain, which we must now suffer from the pagans: it was not thought possible that such havoc could have been made. Behold the church of St Cuthbert, spattered with the blood of the priests of God, miserably despoiled of all its ornaments.'

Alongside this can be set the dramatic words from the *Anglo-Saxon Chronicle*: '793. In this year terrible portents appeared in Northumbria, and miserably afflicted the inhabitants: these were exceptional flashes of lightning, and fiery dragons were seen flying in the air, and soon followed a great famine, and after that in the same year the harrying of the heathen miserably destroyed God's church in Lindisfarne by rapine and slaughter.'

Not all took such a gloomy view of the Vikings, however. Some years after the raids, it was recorded that English women favoured Vikings because they took baths on Saturdays, combed their hair, and wore fine clothing. These habits were not universally admired, however – the tenth-century Arab writer Ibn Fadlan, describing Scandinavian traders, was disgusted by them, 'They are the dirtiest of God's creatures . . . and they do not wash themselves after sex.'

The Viking as heroic warrior was preserved for posterity in the writings of Icelandic poets, some three centuries after the events they described. The sagas were part of a tradition not unlike that of the American 'Wild West', which glorified even as it sometimes condemned the exploits of the Norse equivalents of Billy the Kid.

In the past twenty years there has been a concerted effort on the part of historians and archaeologists to find a more balanced view of the period. The Vikings have been argued as no more bloodthirsty than most of their contemporaries, and as well as warriorship there were Viking career prospects as administrators, traders, artists, and lawyers. The English word 'law' notably comes from a Scandinavian root.

THE ORIGINS OF THE VIKINGS

The word 'Viking' may derive from a word meaning 'away from home', but by the time Viking exploits were being set down in Iceland the word 'vikingr' meant 'warrior' or 'pirate', and was therefore not applicable to the majority of Viking-period Scandinavians, who were farmers. The term was not often used in the time of the Viking raids, when the people concerned were known by their country of origin, notably as Danes or Northmen, the Swedes figuring in less high profile in the Western literature.

The period of the Viking raids was one of rapid development in Scandinavia. In their homelands the Northmen were farmers and fishermen who lived in farmsteads and villages. Only a few large settlements, such as the trading base of Helgö in Sweden, had existed since the Migration period. Pressure on land in Scandinavia probably increased as a result of population explosion. There were many factors behind this – climate was one, changing political and social configurations were others. Light, ocean-going boats made the Viking raids feasible – they were fast, and could easily be turned round for a quick getaway.

THE VIKINGS IN BRITAIN

The Norse were the most adventurous of the seafarers as the sea was in their blood. They colonized parts of Scotland, Ireland, the Isle of Man, and the north of England; they raided but did not colonize Wales. Travelling north and west, they reached the Faeroes, then Iceland and Greenland. From there they went on to discover Vinland (America).

The Danes were the main settlers in south-east England. The Northmen, including the Danes, settled in France and later became the Normans.

For the Swedes eastward expansion seemed preferable. It was they who forged a route to Constantinople and beyond, and who established towns such as Kiev in Russia.

The Vikings were not so successful in the East as they were in the West. The East attracted them, as the Arab world was a ready source of the silver they desired, and the Byzantine Empire was similarly rich. But Arabs and Byzantines were well organized and sophisticated compared to the Northmen. Although on occasions in the tenth century the Vikings joined forces with Slavs from Russia to hassle Byzantium (one carved a runic inscription in Santa Sophia), they fared better in the north-west, where the administrations were weaker and smaller and thus less able to defend themselves.

Despite their image on vellum, the Vikings seem to have been rapidly assimilated into the population of England, to the point where archaeologists have difficulty distinguishing Viking farmsteads from those of Anglo-Saxons, for example. This is especially the case after their conversion to Christianity in the tenth century. There are almost as many problems identifying Christian Viking graves. However, it cannot be argued that the Scandinavian presence is comparatively undetectable in England because it was minor, since placenames alone attest a strong presence.

Elsewhere assimilation was not as rapid, and in the Northern Isles of Scotland and the Isle of Man the Norse retained their culture to a far greater degree.

As was the case with the Anglo-Saxon settlements, the numbers involved in the early Scandinavian raids on Britain may not have been as great as was once believed. The *Anglo-Saxon Chronicle* suggests that the Viking fleets at most numbered just over 80 vessels, and some of the fleets recorded were no more than three. Given that each ship contained about 50 men, or fewer, the largest raiding parties must have comprised less than a thousand men. Estimates of the Danish army vary – current opinion puts it at several thousand men.

The raids began in the late eighth century. Norse were responsible for a raid in 787 which made its landing at Portland in the south of England. Lindisfarne was attacked in 793 – the *Chronicle* states by Danes.

The Danish attack on England was concentrated on the south, between 865 and 954. After this initial period, there was a time of peaceful settlement, then a second phase of aggressive Viking activity. The course of the raids is documented in the *Anglo-Saxon Chronicle*. The turning point seems to have been in 835, when a Danish army wintered for the first time in England, heralding a more serious programme of concerted attack. Between 865 and 880 campaigns by the Danes led to much of Northumbria, east Mercia and east Anglia falling into their hands, with the temporary seizure of London and inroads being made into Wessex.

THE DANELAW

It is at this point that Alfred the Great entered the scene, successfully repulsing the Danish advance, and establishing a territorial divide along the line of Watling Steet (which ran from Chester through Lichfield to Bedford and London), the region to its east being the Danelaw. The division was effected in the Treaty of Wedmore in 878, agreed between Alfred and the Danish leader Guthrum. West of this line control was in the hands of an ealdorman who had married Alfred's daughter Aethelflaeda.

The Danelaw became a Danish region which had a marked effect on the future development of England, arguably even eventually contributing to the so-called modern 'north–south divide'. Within it the Danes established the 'Five Boroughs', Nottingham, Lincoln, Stamford, Derby, and Leicester, which were major trading centres. In the Danelaw, as the name suggests, Danish law and language prevailed.

In the north, Danish influence was not felt very strongly, but here the key figures were the Norse, or more precisely the Norse-Irish, who had come

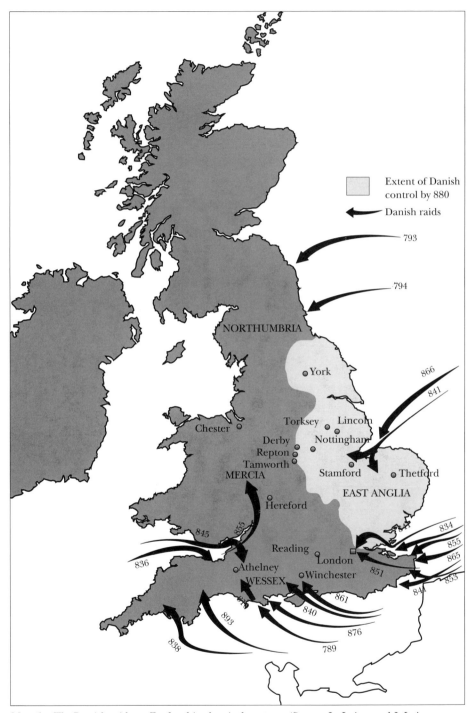

Map 6. The Danish raids on England in the ninth century. (Source: L. Laing and J. Laing,
Anglo-Saxon England, *Map 3.)*

from Ireland and established themselves first in the west, around Chester and the Wirral, then east of the Pennines in Yorkshire. York, which had been an Anglian town, became first Danish and then Norse. It reverted to the English by 927.

Alfred died in 899, having established his kingdom of Wessex as the most important in England. His son Edward the Elder began the work of reclaiming England from the Danes, abetted by his sister Aethelflaeda, who had inherited Mercia from her now deceased ealdorman husband. A pattern of attrition returned lost lands in Mercia and in Essex and Hertfordshire. By 920 all England south of the Humber was once more in English hands. In that year at Bakewell in Derbyshire Raegnald, the ruler of the Vikings of York, submitted to Edward, as did the Northumbrians, the Strathclyde Britons, and the Scots.

Edward's successor Aethelstan ruled both Danes and Saxons, successfully campaigning in the north, and becoming the first king of all England. It was a short period of triumph, for on his death two years after securing his kingdom the second Viking age began.

Aethelstan's successors were far less glorious. Edward the Martyr was murdered, and was followed in 978 by Aethelred II, the Unready (meaning 'unwilling to accept advice'). During Aethelred's reign Danish attacks were renewed, the most important leader being Swein Forkbeard, who had driven his own father Harald of Denmark out of his lands and conducted a couple of swift raids on England before a campaign in earnest which started in 1013. Having landed in England, he made his base near Gainsborough in Lincolnshire, and was hailed king by the Northumbrians and the Danelaw Danes. His army marched south into Mercia, then Wessex. Here he accepted the surrender of Winchester and Oxford. London surrendered to him later in 1013. He died soon after, and was succeeded by his son Cnut. Aethelred had fled the country on the fall of London, but now returned. Cnut returned briefly to Denmark, but was soon back with a huge army that campaigned first against Aethelred then against his son Edmund Ironside. At Ashingdon, in Essex, Cnut was victorious, and in 1016 became the first Danish king of England.

Cnut was an able ruler, who also became king of Denmark and then of Norway. He maintained a standing army and a fleet, and devised a law code

Fig. 16. Viking bone plaques, Continental and British. Left: North Norway. Right: Scar, Sanday, Orkney.

based on that of the Anglo-Saxons. On his death in 1035 a period of uncertainty ended with the rule of the Anglo-Saxon king Edward the Confessor, who was crowned in 1043. Anglo-Saxon control of England, however, was brief, and ended in 1066 with the Norman Conquest.

THE NORSE IN CELTIC LANDS

While the Danes were making their presence felt in England, the Norse were active in Scotland.

The northern Scottish kingdoms of the Picts and the Scots had been united around 843 under a Scottic leader, Kenneth mac Alpin. Christianity spread from Iona to Pictland between the sixth and early eighth centuries, and Irish monks, known as Papae, were to be found in the Northern Isles at the time of the Viking settlements.

Although it has been suggested that some graves in Scotland (such as that at Lamlash in Arran) may date from the late eighth century, there is no real evidence for Norse activity before the early years of the ninth, and older objects in some Norse graves may simply be heirlooms. Iona was raided in the early years of the ninth century, and the settlement of the Northern Isles probably began not long after. The main source of information concerning it is the *Orkneyinga Saga*, set down in Iceland long after the events it describes. The saga asserts that the opponents of Harald Harfagri were driven out of Norway after the battle of Hafrsfjord; it erroneously dates this battle too early. The story relates how Harald pursued his enemies in Shetland and Orkney, then went on to colonize the Isle of Man before returning to Orkney to found a Norse earldom. Certainly Orkney remained a Norse earldom from the ninth century onwards, when Earl Sigurd the Mighty ruled it, though it later became subject to the king of Norway. The earldom persisted until the thirteenth century and the conversion of the Norse to Christianity took place under Earl Thorfinn in the eleventh century.

From the northern base the Western Isles were colonized, and used as stepping stones for the colonization of the Isle of Man. The Isle of Man was ideally placed in the 'Celtic Mediterranean' for raids on the adjacent coasts – south-west Scotland, Wales, and Ireland. Galloway seems to have been settled at a secondary stage by Norse–Irish.

ARCHAEOLOGY AND THE VIKING RAIDS

The archaeological records of the Vikings consist primarily of coins, fortifications, settlements, and burials.

Viking fortifications were put up during the raids when it was found necessary to establish winter camps. The most extensively investigated is that at Repton, Derbyshire, where the Vikings wintered in 873/4. They incorporated the Anglo-Saxon church within the curve of their earthworks, which formed a D-shaped enclosure on the bank of the River Trent. Outside the enclosure were found, interred in a disused stone building, the remains of 250 bodies, seemingly moved there from elsewhere, since the skeletons were not articulated and the skulls had been stacked on the top of the pile of bones. Most were of men between their late teens and their forties – they outnumbered women 4 to 1. Coins and other objects found with them indicated that they had been buried in the Viking period, and the coins were in keeping with a date in the later 870s. None showed any signs of injury, so presumably they cannot be claimed as evidence for Viking brutality. Other burials near the church seem to have been of Viking warriors. One, who clearly met a violent end, was buried in a wooden coffin with a sword in a fleece-lined wooden scabbard, a folding knife, a silver charm, beads, buckles, and a boar's tooth.

What has been identified as a Viking fortification has also been found at the Udal, in North Uist. Built in the mid-ninth century, it was replaced in the tenth or eleventh by an undefended open settlement. Other defended sites have been identified as probably the work of the Danes, but have not been tested by excavation.

Comparatively little is known about the homes of the first Viking settlers in England. Most information comes from the upland areas, where an increasing number of abandoned farmsteads have been recognized, though without excavation they cannot be assigned with certainty to this period. However, two excavated settlements have been shown to belong to this period. The first, at Ribblehead in North Yorkshire, stands on an exposed limestone pavement, and comprises a farmyard with three buildings, a longhouse, a bakery, and a smithy. The occupants lived at a level barely above subsistence, although four copper coins of the ninth century showed some contact with the outside world. At Simy Folds in County Durham three sites had single stone-built houses with adjacent subsidiary buildings, arranged in each case round a yard. The occupants farmed sheep, cattle, and pigs, and cultivated cereals, during the Viking period, although again the finds were few, and it is difficult to be certain whether the occupants were Vikings or Anglo-Saxons. The same comment applies to Bryant's Gill in Cumbria, where once again a longhouse was the focus of a subsistence-level farm. The evidence from Cumbria points to extensive colonization of the wastelands of the central Lake District, probably in the tenth century, when Hiberno-Norse were driven out of Ireland. Nine out of ten placenames in this region are of Scandinavian origin, though some elements suggest a mixed population, including people from the Faeroes, Iceland, Ireland, the Isle of Man, and probably the Hebrides.

More information about Viking-period settlements comes from the Isle of

Man and from Scotland. In the Isle of Man it is once again difficult to be certain from finds whether the farmsteads belonged to Viking settlers or to natives, since the longhouse seems to have been widely adopted in Britain at this time. Most interesting among the Manx sites are promontory forts (often these are re-used Iron Age sites), which may have been bases for raids. Cronk ny Merriu, Cass ny Hawin, and Close ny Chollagh all have longhouses within their defences, and at Vowlan a naturally defended promontory was occupied by six successive timber houses with Norse-style plans.

It is, however, in the Northern Isles that Viking settlement can best be studied. The classic site is Jarlshof on Sumburgh Head in Shetland. Here a succession of prehistoric settlements were succeeded by Norse occupation which extended from the ninth to the twelfth centuries. Jarlshof started out as a single 'parent' farmstead. The property consisted of a longhouse built of stones collected from the beach, with two rooms, a kitchen and a living room. The main entrance led into the kitchen, in the centre of which was a rectangular hearth with an oven or cooking pit. In the living room there were low benches along the walls on the top of which tables or beds would have been placed. Beyond the main farmhouse lay the outbuildings – smithy, byre, barn, and outhouse. Nearby was what has been interpreted as either a temple or bath-house. The settlers farmed sheep, pigs, cattle, and ponies, and also practised some agriculture. Their diet was supplemented by a limited amount of fishing. Most of the objects that were needed by the farm were made on the site, bone being fashioned into a variety of items, including combs and pins. The inhabitants used soapstone which could easily be carved into pots – the earliest may have been fashioned from pieces imported from Norway, but they soon found a local source. The original farmstead was extended in the later ninth and again in the tenth century, when fishing and seal hunting became particularly important.

A number of other Viking settlements are known from the Northern Isles, such as the farmstead at Underhoull in Shetland and the settlements at Skaill, Orphir, Birsay, and Buckquoy in Orkney. The walling of Viking-period houses in the Northern Isles displayed an early form of cavity wall insulation, with a turf core and inner and outer stone facing. They were slightly bow-sided, often with pairs of opposed doors set eccentrically in the long sides. Similar houses are known in the Western Isles.

Perhaps the most interesting Viking houses are those recently excavated at Whithorn in Galloway. Built of wood, the remains were very well preserved due to waterlogging. This settlement was established around AD 1000 and comprised a group of single-roomed houses, each with a central stone-built hearth and a paved pathway from door to centre. On either side were benches for beds. The community appears to have been a small trading post, and there is evidence for the working of iron, copper, lead, antler, and leather.

VIKING COIN HOARDS

One of the most useful indicators of Viking raids and settlement is the study of coin hoards. Hoards are fairly sparse for the period prior to 850, but from 865 onwards they are more abundant, and comprise mostly Anglo-Saxon coins, either buried by the potential victim in fear of attack, or by Vikings hiding their loot. The hoards are usually identifiable from the fact that they contain a mass of hacksilver, pieces of armlets, brooches, or even ingots destined for the melting pot. They often contain Arab dirhems, as these were one of the main sources of Viking silver and were redistributed through north-west Europe by Viking agency. The earliest occurrence of these issues in hoards is in one from Croydon, deposited in the 870s, although there is a stray find from the trading site of Hamwic of pre-Viking date. The largest of the Viking hoards is that from Cuerdale, Lancs – 88 lb (40 kg) of silver (including 1,000 ingots and 7,500 coins) were deposited in a lead chest around AD 905. Another tenth-century hoard with Arab coins is that found at Skaill, Orkney, which contained typical 'thistle' brooches (penannular brooches with brambled terminals and pins). These hoards also usually contain silver armlets or rings, which probably served as a form of currency.

VIKING RELIGION

The original Viking settlers were pagans, who worshipped a variety of gods and goddesses, essentially the same as those of the pagan Anglo-Saxons before them. Conversion to Christianity was erratic – Guthrum, the Danish leader, was converted by Alfred in 878 – but after their conversion, some converts seem to have hedged their bets, choosing to be buried in Christian churchyards with their swords.

Even after the conversion of the Vikings, some of the pagan stories continued to be carved on crosses, perhaps being adapted to convey Christian messages. Among pagan myths represented on cross-slabs are representations of the story of Wayland the Smith, and Sigurd, who roasted the heart of the dragon Fafnir, burnt his thumb and in sucking it acquired extrasensory perception.

VIKING BURIALS

Graves of the pagan Vikings are often very distinctive. Many different burial customs are known from Britain, often reflecting Scandinavian traditions, but others apparently displaying features distinctive of the local area. The most noteworthy form of interment is the ship burial, although this is comparatively rare. It is represented in Orkney, in the Hebrides, and in the Isle of Man. One of the richest ship burials was found in the nineteenth century at Kiloran Bay, Colonsay. It contained the body of a man accompanied by his sword, shield, spear, axe, harness gear, and a set of scales and weights. Two male burials at Westness on Rousay were laid in boats 4.5 and 5.5 m long, respectively, with a burial chamber demarcated by large stones in the centre of each. These boats were laid in trenches in the ground without any covering mound, but other boat burials were more clearly demarcated, sometimes by mounds, such as at Knock-y-Doonee on the Isle of Man. There are signs of unusual burial practices on a few sites. At Ballateare on the Isle of Man the mound covering the burial seems to have been made from turves brought from different locations. One suggestion was that a turf had been cut from each of the fields owned by the dead man. The same burial mound contained in its upper part a female burial with the back of the skull sliced off. The same feature seems to be attested at the Balladoole burial site, suggesting that these misfortunes were no accidents but ritual sacrifices.

Most Viking burials in the British Isles are inhumations, but cremations were represented in the Danish cemetery at Ingleby in Derbyshire. A funeral fire was detected on the site of another burial at Hesket-in-Forest in Lancashire, although the accompanying objects seem to have been placed in the grave after the fire.

Apart from these and other isolated Viking burials, such as that found at Sonning in Sussex, cemeteries have been recorded, for example at Pierowall in Orkney. The pagan Vikings were buried with characteristic gravegoods – women's burials, in particular, are usually accompanied by distinctive 'tortoise' brooches.

THE IMPACT OF THE VIKINGS ON BRITAIN

In many ways the greatest significance of the Viking episode was that it served as a catalyst in the development of English society – English culture became more English when juxtaposed with the culture of its adversaries.

There has been much debate about the extent to which the Vikings were responsible for major changes in English society, and to what extent these were already under way and were simply accelerated by the Scandinavian settlements. In particular, the question of town development in the late Saxon period has attracted attention.

The idea of town development, so enthusiastically espoused by Alfred the Great, was taken up by the Vikings, who were responsible for the growth of the Five Boroughs which were the economic centres of the Danelaw. Some of the Danelaw towns grew to be of considerable size – Lincoln and Norwich had populations of over 5,000.

These were not new towns as such since there had previously been Anglo-Saxon *burhs* on the sites. The Vikings defended them as fortresses, but their role in developing urban life within them is less clear. There is no doubt, however, that the Vikings stimulated their growth, as they prompted the development of another key town of the late Saxon period – Jorvik (York).

JORVIK

The Viking remains at York have been substantially well preserved through waterlogging, which conserves organic material that otherwise seldom survives. The Anglo-Saxon predecessor of Jorvik, known as *Eoforwic*, was in decline in the early ninth century before it was revitalized by the Vikings. Around 900 the old defensive system (basically that of Roman Eboracum, the predecessor of the Anglo-Saxon town) was refurbished, an earth bank being constructed with a palisade on its crest which ran down to the rivers Ouse and Foss. The defences enclosed a total area of 36 ha, making it larger than even the major Swedish towns that have been excavated. By the eleventh century Jorvik was a major city with wide trading networks, particularly with Denmark.

These trade contacts are indicated by amber from the Baltic, steatite bowls from Shetland, a Pictish brooch from northern Scotland, pottery from Germany, and stones from different sources in northern England and Scotland. Walrus ivory presumably came from Norway.

Outside the areas of England in which towns already existed at the time of the Viking settlements, the Scandinavians were not major town builders. The only exception to this pattern was in Ireland, where they developed Dublin and founded other centres at Cork and Waterford.

OVERSEAS TRADE

Despite the Scandinavian trading patterns in north-west Europe as a whole, overseas trade in the Viking age was relatively minor. Out of some 15,000 ninth-century objects found in the Viking levels at Coppergate, York, only 500 were imported, and in the tenth-century levels almost the only finds of an exotic character were a silk cap, a brooch from the Low Countries, and a German storage vessel. No Scandinavian pottery turned up in the 55,000 Viking-period pieces from the site. However, walrus ivory, soapstone, and schist, used in making whetstones, were imported from Scandinavia, or, in the case of the soapstone, possibly from Shetland. Most of the items could have been objects not traded but brought over by Scandinavian settlers. Silk has been identified not only at York but at Lincoln (where it could have come from the same bale as that in York), and London.

LANGUAGE

Considerable debate has centred on the extent of the Scandinavian settlement. The consensus of opinion, however, is that the influx was

Plate 1. Ceremonial jadeite axes from Cunzierton, Roxburghshire. Made from stone probably imported from Switzerland or the Alps. These were deliberately buried in a Neolithic ritual in the third millennium BC. (© Trustees of the National Museums of Scotland, 1995)

Plate 2. Beaker decorated with cord-impressed patterns inlaid with white paint, Fingask, Perthshire. Beakers of various types were widespread in Western Europe at the end of the third millennium BC, and appear to represent an intrusive tradition in Britain which may have been partly introduced by immigrants. (© Trustees of the National Museums of Scotland, 1995)

Plate 3. Silver cup of an Iron Age chieftain of the first century AD at Welwyn, Herts. It was probably made in Italy at the time of the Emperor Augustus. Such objects represent high status gift exchange or trade between the Iron Age Celts and the Roman world before the Roman conquest by Claudius. (© British Museum)

Plate 4. This detail from a Roman floor mosaic of the second century AD from Cirencester, Glos., depicts Actaeon being turned into a stag by the goddess Diana. The same mosaic shows personifications of the four seasons, demonstrating how Roman civilization had been assimilated by Britain. (© Corinium Museum, Cirencester)

Plate 5. Reconstructed gateway of the Roman fort at South Shields, Tyne and Wear. The Roman army was the main instrument of Romanization in Britain, and forts were built partly to impress the British Celts with the Roman presence. (© Lloyd Laing)

Plate 6. Walls of the Saxon Shore fort at Portchester, Hants, still stand furnished with bastions for catapults much as they did in the fourth century AD. Later used as the curtain wall of a Norman castle, the site proclaims the military might of two separate European incomers. (© Jenny Laing)

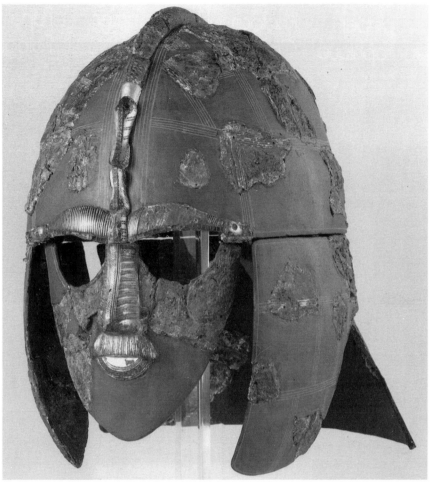

Plate 7. Reconstructed from many fragments, this parade helmet was found in the Anglo-Saxon royal burial, Sutton Hoo, Suffolk. It displays Swedish characteristics and was probably imported from Sweden, reflecting the European origins of the East Anglian royal dynasty. (© British Museum)

Plate 8. Unique among the coins issued by Offa, Anglo-Saxon king of Mercia, 757–96, this gold dinar bears inscriptions in Arabic. It bears the Mohammedan date of AH 157 (AD 773–4), and appears to have been inspired by a coin issued by Caliph al-Mansur. It may have been part of an annual gift to the pope, though it may also have been intended for trade with Spain. (© British Museum)

Plate 9. The tower of the Anglo-Saxon church at Earl's Barton, Northamptonshire. Arguably the finest late Saxon tower to survive, its arcading may reflect Continental Carolingian influence. Late tenth century. (© Jenny Laing)

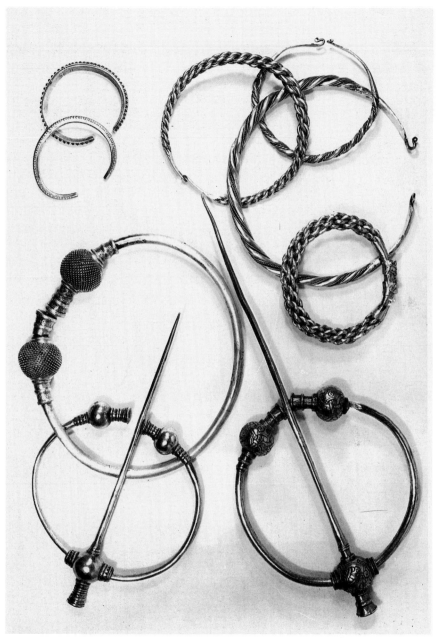

Plate 10. Finds from a Viking silver hoard found at Skaill, Mainland, Orkney in 1858. Dating from the late tenth century, it included Arabic silver coins and an Anglo-Saxon penny of Aethelstan. The 'thistle' brooches shown here include one decorated in an indigenous version of the Scandinavian Jellinge style. (© Trustees of the National Museums of Scotland)

Plate 11. Southwell Minster, Notts. Started before 1114 in the French-derived Romanesque style, it gives a particularly clear impression of the original appearance of Romanesque churches. The spires are an 1880 restoration of the original lead-covered wooden ones destroyed in 1711. The Perpendicular window is a later medieval addition. (© Jenny Laing)

Plate 12. Medieval jug from Kidwelly, Carmarthen, imported from the Saintonge region of France in the late thirteenth century. Decorated with paint on an off-white ground, such jugs were probably imported to Britain as part of the trade which brought French wine. (© National Museums of Wales)

Plate 13. Harlech Castle. Begun in 1283 this is one of a series of castles designed on a concentric plan by the Savoyard architect Master James of St George for Edward I's campaigns in Wales. Drawn by Sir Richard Colt Hoare in the early nineteenth century.

Plate 14. Chiswick House, Middlesex, built 1725–9 in the neo-classical Palladian style originally developed by the sixteenth-century Italian architect Palladio. The house is the work of the architect William Kent for Lord Burlington, the foremost patron of the style. (© English Heritage)

substantial, and rapidly led to mixed blood, since Scandinavian laws were relatively loose about arrangements for cohabiting and marriage. In later medieval times it was accepted that the Scandinavians had made an important contribution to society. Gerald of Wales was of the view that the Welsh skill in part singing was due to a Scandinavian legacy, and that the same phenomenon accounted for musical skills in the north-east of England.

Old Norse, the language spoken by the incomers, was not dissimilar to Anglo-Saxon, both being Teutonic. In the thirteenth century, an Icelandic writer commented that the language of England prior to the introduction of French by the Normans was one and the same as the language spoken in Norway and Denmark. The differences between the two are more apparent now, probably because Old Norse in the form in which it survives is comparatively late. The language spoken in England in 1100 was Anglo-Scandinavian, and this fact is even apparent in the writings of such English clerics as Wulfstan of York (archbishop 1002–23) whose English was fundamentally the correct dialect of Wessex, the equivalent of modern 'BBC English'. Old Norse was the language of runic inscriptions, which were still carved in parts of Britain (including in Carlisle Cathedral) down to the mid-twelfth century. However, rather than literary English becoming corrupted by Norse, Old Norse became corrupted by English. It would certainly have been understood, however, in the Danelaw until well after the Norman Conquest.

English borrowed a great deal from Old Norse, particularly in its spoken form. The process went on from the time of the Scandinavian settlements until the twelfth century, enriching the language with words that can be found on almost every page of this book. Among common nouns are: bank, knife, midden, bond, scowl, sky, calf, egg, fellow, boulder, harbour, husband, window, kid, anger, band, outlaw, rake, scrap, bread, cake, sneer, boon, stack, stump, filly, gift, hank, and wing. Verbs include: to call, to take, to die, and to happen. Other words include: score, scuffle, fling, gasp, bleak, tangle, tatter, dangle, their, them, though, cast, raise, ransack, doze, ski, skin, skip, thrift, thrive, ugly, dawn, aloft, slush, sneer, spray, big, get, hit, jolly, lurk, nag, weak, muggy, odd, prod, craze, reef, root, rotten, rub, scream, scold, guess, haggle, scorch, skirt, slang, grovel, happy, slant, swirl, stagger, tipple, twiddle, and whim.

Among the many personal names that may have originated with the Vikings are: Baynes, Bland, Bond, Brenner, Briggs, Carman, Coles, Drake, Drummond, Fell, Fellows, Foote, Gill, Gunnell, Hackett, Haldane, Haskell, Haynes, Hemming, Kay, Keays, Kerr, Kydd, Legge, Macaulay, Myers, Orr, Osborn, Osmond, Ravenhill, Reynolds, Scarfe, Schofield, Skinner, Sotheby, Spratling, Storr, Tait, Thacker, Todd, Turk, Withers and Wragg.

The influence of Scandinavian language is most apparent in the areas of law and administration. 'Law' itself, words such as outlaw, earl, and thrall, and technical legal terms such as grith (peace) are all borrowings from Norse.

PLACENAMES

Placenames are a major source for studying the Scandinavian impact on Britain. Scandinavian names abound in the region to the east of the line drawn in the agreement between Alfred and Guthrum at Wedmore. To the west of this line, with the exception of a few stray names in Warwickshire and Northamptonshire, they are extremely rare. To the east and north of the line, however, they mostly predominate, although in Northumberland and Durham to the north and in Essex and Hertfordshire in the south, they are very much rarer. There are a few areas where Norse, as opposed to Danish, names occur – this is the case in Wirral and Lancashire, settled by Norse–Irish, and in Yorkshire, where Nidderdale, Calderdale, and Craven display a similar wealth of Norwegian elements. Not surprisingly, the richest concentrations are in the area of the Five Boroughs, and in Yorkshire, though less in the West Riding.

Some placename elements provide clues to the nature of the settlements. Names with the element *-by* represent settlements established by the Danes on the best farmland in the years following the campaigns of the 860s and 870s. *-By* placenames are also found densely distributed in the Lincolnshire Wolds, which seem to have been settled by movement inland from the Humber. Many of the *-by* names incorporate a Danish personal name, marking early inroads in the ninth century. The same root gives the term 'by-laws' which means 'laws of the village'. Examples are Hundleby (Hundulf's village), Swarby (Svarri's village), and Walesby (Val's village).

-Thorp placenames seem to represent a secondary stage in the Scandinavian settlement, and again many are early and combined with Danish names. They are concentrated in Yorkshire, in areas of sheep farming. Examples of this type of name are Foggathorpe (Folkvarth's hamlet) and Winthorpe (Wina's hamlet).

A particular type of name is the 'Grimston hybrid', which combined a Danish personal name with the English ending *-tun*. It has been suggested that these names, which are particularly to be found in Nottinghamshire and Leicestershire, represent lordships taken over by Danish military leaders in the early stages of the settlement.

In Scotland, Norse placenames abound in the Northern Isles. It has been calculated that there are at least 50,000 placenames of Scandinavian origin in Shetland, and that 99 per cent of all Orkney farm names are Norse in origin. The language of Orkney was Norn, and this persisted through the sixteenth and into the seventeenth century, although in the eighteenth century it was replaced by English. In Shetland, however, Norn lasted longer. Around 1600 a minister on the remote island of Unst went to Norway to learn Norwegian, so that he could be understood by his congregation, and in the 1890s more than 10,000 words and phrases that had been used in living memory were collected by researchers. Among the placenames of Scandinavian origin in the Northern Isles *-bister* names are particularly common, from *bolstadr*, a farm, as in Isbister or Braebister, and *-setter* names also abound, from *setr*, a house or homestead, as in Grimsetter or Voxter.

Elsewhere in Scotland the evidence is not as clear. Scandinavian and Gaelic languages seem to have existed side by side in the Western Isles until at least the thirteenth century. Most of the Gaelic placenames of the Western Isles are of Viking-period origin – in Lewis this is particularly the case, but even in Skye about 60 per cent of the names contain Norse elements. A similar story is told by the placenames of the Isle of Man.

INSTITUTIONS

Although the underlying administrative divisions of England in the time of the Vikings were those of the Anglo-Saxons, the large counties of Lincolnshire and Yorkshire were divided into what the Scandinavians called *trithings*, which has given the term Ridings in Yorkshire. The shires were subdivided into hundreds, each with its own court, but in the Danelaw the divisions were known as *wappentakes*, from a word for the brandishing of swords at an assembly. Although the word was Anglicized, it was favoured in the Danelaw to the equivalent hundred.

The Danes were very litigious, with a healthy respect for the law that belies their reputation. In 962 King Edgar allowed the Danes to exercise their secular rights 'according to the good law they can best decide upon', and Ethelred II made a statement at Wantage (in Wessex) which defined a code of law for the men of the Five Boroughs to be set alongside the 'law of the English'.

Land transactions, in particular, were subject to different rules in the Danelaw, where a system of dependence on sureties (called *festermen*) was employed. Similarly, it seems that the Danelaw had a public prosecutor (*sacrabar*), and this office seems to have also held jurisdiction in parts of Cheshire.

In the Danelaw the methods of assessing fines and penalties were different, and different terms were used for currency. Methods of measuring land were distinctively Scandinavian; in the Danelaw it was assessed in terms of *carucates*, *oxgangs* and *bovates*. The Danelaw 'ploughland' was the amount of soil that could be tilled by one plough-team in a year.

The social structure of the peasantry had different elements in the Danelaw, where the *sokeman* was the equivalent of the villein elsewhere. All these variations had a legacy for the later Middle Ages.

In the Isle of Man the Norse had an enormous impact on the institutions. Here the land divisions were of Norse origin, as is the House of Keys (the Manx parliament). The folk moot, or thing, was held at a mound at Tynwald – the same placename evidence accounts for Dingwall in northern Scotland. The House of Keys has the twenty-four seats of its Scandinavian origin – originally it was the parliament for the Isle of Man and the Western Isles, and had thirty-two seats, but these were reduced after the Western Isles broke free in part in 1156.

VIKING ART

The most obvious contribution of the Vikings to British culture is in the field of art. Although sharing similar roots and a similar liking for stylized animal ornament, after the Conversion Anglo-Saxon art grew more in line with Christian humanist traditions, and developed along somewhat different lines from that in Scandinavia. The barbarian Viking art styles made the English in the heartlands of the south more conscious of their 'civilized' values, and the artists of Wessex, in particular, turned to the Carolingian world for inspiration. The result was the humanistic art of the Winchester School, perhaps the greatest single English contribution to European art.

Scandinavian art styles, however, penetrated far beyond the limits of the areas settled by the Vikings, and persisted even after the Norman Conquest, as the tendrils of Viking Urnes style ornament adorning the Norman church at Kilpeck in Hereford can testify.

The Scandinavian incomers brought over a variety of objects decorated in the styles current in their homelands, and these were rapidly taken up in Britain, where, in due course, native versions were developed.

The earliest of the Viking styles found in Britain is known as Borre, after a grave in Norway. This style was fashionable in the ninth/tenth centuries, and is well represented at York and in Dublin. Its characteristic motif is a kind of ring-chain pattern, and it is found on both metalwork and sculpture, such as the famous Gosforth Cross in Cumbria.

The next style was the Jellinge, named after a silver cup with this kind of decoration found in Denmark. In England it was fashionable in the tenth century, and is typified by an animal with double outline. A school of sculpture seems to have operated at York producing Jellinge ornament of fairly mediocre quality. The style is found almost exclusively in Yorkshire and Teesside.

The Viking-influenced sculpture of the north of England is extremely copious, and for the most part displays elements of both Anglo-Saxon and Scandinavian traditions. Christian subject matter is combined with elements from Scandinavian mythology, showing how far the pagan and Christian elements seem to have been fused together in Christian imagery.

Most of the sculpture in the north of England belongs to the later ninth and tenth centuries. The later Viking styles, found in the south, are barely represented.

Of the later styles, the first is Ringerike, current in the eleventh century. The tendril-like ornament bears some similarity to the acanthus foliage patterns fashionable in Wessex and the Carolingian world, which may account for the acceptance of the new style in the south – classic among the relatively few known examples of pure Ringerike is a tombstone from St Paul's churchyard, London, which has a Viking runic inscription. Ringerike was fashionable in the Norse colonies in Scotland, and a native version of the related Mammen style can be seen on a fine silver brooch from a hoard at Skaill and in a lion carving in a prehistoric tomb at Maes Howe, both in Orkney.

A final Scandinavian style which had considerable impact on Celtic artists in Ireland, but was less popular in England, was the Urnes, named after a carving on a wooden church in Norway. Urnes style employed elongated tendrils, and appears mostly after the Norman Conquest, particularly in manuscripts, though on occasion in sculpture, such as in the Crucifixion scene at Jevington, Sussex.

CHAPTER SIX

The Normans and the Early Middle Ages

On Saturday 14 October 1066, after preparations of less than a year, William of Normandy 'conquered' England in a single day – 'between the third hour and evening', chronicled the medieval writer William of Poitiers. Naturally, consolidating this achievement took somewhat longer, but essentially those few hours enabled the Normans to sweep away, change, modify, or adapt much that had been established under the Romans, Saxons, and Vikings. Once more the intervention of Europe arrested and enveloped what had been developing into distinctively insular styles. Many features introduced by the Normans still exist today. A new royal line was established, which was to last into the twelfth century, a new aristocracy of Norman French origin was put in place, and similarly the Anglo-Saxon clergy were led by Normans. By 1090 only one of the sixteen bishoprics in England was held by an Englishman, while in the time of Domesday Book (1086) fewer than six of the 180 great landlords and tenants-in-chief were English. Virtually all land was either held by the king, or by a handful of his supporters who had come with him from France. This system remains today, since technically any property 'owner' is the tenant (ultimately of the Crown), in contrast to the outright ownership enjoyed in Europe.

As has been claimed with all previous conquests, however, the take-over was definitely mainly at the top. There were, of course, settlements of Normans in England, particularly in the Welsh borders and in 'French' quarters in towns, and conversely there was a limited amount of population drift from England to Normandy, but the population of England for the most part remained English, even though they adjusted to Norman ways. It has been estimated that there were about 10,000 incoming Normans at most, with a surviving Anglo-Saxon population of 1.5–2.5 million. Analysis of the bodies in a cemetery at St Helen's-on-the-Walls in York, however, suggests that there was a change in the physical type of the people buried there around the Norman conquest, reflected in the cranial shape. Thus far, the explanation has eluded archaeologists.

THE NORMANS IN EUROPE

Who were these Norman conquerors? The story of their rise in Europe is one of the most remarkable in medieval history, since the Norman episode was of remarkably short duration.

In origin, the Normans were Vikings. Their story begins with the appearance of longships on the Seine, the great waterway that gave access to the heart of France. Viking pirates were first recorded terrorizing the Franks on the Seine in the middle of the ninth century, and by 911 they had proved so successful in their military endeavours that to buy peace Charles the Simple, king of France, gave them land on the lower Seine, under their leader Rollo.

Little is known of what happened in the newly formed Normandy during the tenth century – as was to be the case the following century in England. It is likely that the Northmen or Normans were a minority who took over at the top.

Research has suggested that the old Carolingian estates were not divided up among the new Norman rulers, but were taken over in their entirety, and indeed, there are signs that the break-up of the Carolingian land-divisions was slower in Normandy than elsewhere.

Archaeology has produced few remains of the Viking activity in Normandy. Only one grave has been found fitted out in Viking fashion (at Pitres), and stray finds have been notably sparse. The presence of Scandinavian coins in Normandy tells us little, for such coins were common throughout north-west Europe. The only conclusion that can be drawn from this is that the incoming population was small, and rapidly assumed the local culture.

The Norman dukes married local women – none had Scandinavian wives. And by the early eleventh century it seems that the overlords had been completely assimilated into the region, developing a new 'Norman' culture that owed much more to the Roman and Frankish past than to any Scandinavian traditions.

In one respect, however, the Normans retained something of their Viking traditions. They were ruthless fighters, who prided themselves on their powerful army. They were skilled horsemen, and recruited from far afield in France.

In return for their military support, 'foreigners' were given lands in Normandy, and many of the Norman nobility in the time of Hastings were knights of only one generation's standing.

This policy of 'drafting in' was also followed in the Norman Church, which along with the army and the state administration was of fundamental importance in the Norman rise to power. The process of strengthening the Church began in 1001 when Duke Richard II established a monastery at Fécamp under William of Volpiano, an Italian monk who had served in the great monastery at Cluny.

Two major figures in the medieval Church were incomers to Normandy and subsequently to England – Lanfranc, an Italian monk who went to a poor community at Bec, and another Italian who came to Bec, Anselm of Aosta. Both became archbishops of Canterbury.

The Normans were their own best publicists. From the beginning of the eleventh century onwards, they commissioned historical narratives intended to stress their cultural and political identity. In this respect they were not unlike their Viking forebears, who, as has been seen, built up a mythology of Viking derring-do long after the events described were over. The Normans, however, used more contemporaneous material, which was manipulated by skilled wordsmiths such as Dudo of Saint-Quentin, William of Jumièges, Orderic Vitalis, and, in England, William of Malmesbury, Henry of Huntingdon, and Ailred of Rievaulx. In the Norman writings, their French background was juxtaposed with their Scandinavian connections, and what they did for Normandy was carefully balanced against the theme of external conquest. In the writings of Dudo, the Normans seem to have had their eye on the conquest of England in the 1020s, claiming that a certain 'Alstelmus' of England, in gratitude for his

Map 7.   The Norman Conquest of England. (Source: T. Rowley, The Norman Heritage *(London, Routledge, 1983), Fig. 10.)*

help, gave half his kingdom to Rollo who subsequently gave it back. Dudo asserted that the Norman duke had the English 'obediently subject to him' and that 'the Scots and Irish ruled under his protection'. This was nonsense, but an insidious nonsense not entirely divorced from the realities of ambition. In 1002 Ethelred the Unready had married Emma, the daughter of Duke Richard II of Normandy, and thus paved the way for the events leading to the conquest of England.

THE NORMAN CONQUEST OF ENGLAND

William's claim to the English throne can be traced back to the marriage of Emma, the wife of Ethelred II. Their son Edward (the Confessor) spent half his life in exile in Normandy and, once he had attained the English throne, introduced Norman advisors and customs to his court. It seems very likely that Edward had decided in the early 1050s that Duke William was to succeed him. On the death of the Confessor, William found himself no longer regarded as the rightful successor in England. In particular he was opposed by Harold Godwinson (a relative by marriage to Edward the Confessor). William prepared for conquest. Harold, briefly Harold II, died in the ensuing battle at Hastings, though probably not by an arrow in the eye, as previously thought.

Local resistance was strong in some areas, particularly the north of England, where a savage campaign between 1068 and 1070 was deemed necessary. 'The Harrying of the North', as it was termed, shocked even Norman loyalists. Simeon of Durham documented the rotting bodies that littered the roads of the region, and records exist of the plague that ensued. Even in Cheshire, by 1070, 162 out of 264 estates were wholly or partially waste. In an entry for 1069 the *Anglo-Saxon Chronicle* bleakly states that William had 'laid waste all the shire' of Yorkshire.

For the best part of a century, historians have debated and failed to reach agreement as to the role of the Normans in European history. Much of the debate has centred on the question of whether major features of Norman culture, such as castles and feudalism, were already fully developed before 1066, or whether they were a response to the conquest, and to what extent England was already strongly linked to the Continent before the Norman invasion.

The Victorians saw the Normans as bringing superior European civilization to a backward Anglo-Saxon England. However, increasingly this century, as both documentary research and archaeology have shed progressive light on later Anglo-Saxon England, it has been suggested that the Normans were not as advanced in many respects as the people they conquered, and that many of the key features of Norman society were the result of assimilation of English ideas. As is so often the case, by the 1960s the pendulum had swung so far away from the idealization of the Normans that any contribution they might have made to English culture was seen as negligible and probably detrimental. Historians now tend towards a different perspective that sees the Norman Conquest as a major catalyst which accelerated trends that might otherwise have taken much longer to develop in England.

In contrast to the situation that prevailed following the Anglo-Saxon settlement of England, there was no reason why the everyday material world of late eleventh-century England should drastically alter. In the fifth century, as was seen above, the decline in urban lifestyle (already apparent before the Anglo-Saxon invasions) was accelerated, and with the demise of towns as viable economic units came the loss of manufacturing and long-distance trade.

In England, the Normans found a flourishing coin-based economy, probably superior to any on the Continent; a thriving tradition of wheel-made pottery, some of it glazed, equal to any found elsewhere in Europe; a sophisticated art; and a pattern of towns and trade upon which they could not improve. There was no large-scale abandonment of villages (except perhaps as a result of the devastation in the north of England) nor the foundation of new, and, as far as can be judged, most rural homes would have looked much the same in 1100 as they would have a century or more previously.

Yet, even though an archaeologist deprived of any documentary evidence might not be able to detect with the trowel any political upheaval from the remains, the impact of the Norman Conquest both in a material and in an ideological way was considerable, and was to be more apparent as time progressed.

CASTLES AND FEUDALISM

It has been said that feudalism was introduced to England in the seventeenth century by Sir Henry Spelman, the historian who first wrote about it. There is some truth in that, for the feudal system that has been seen as the hallmark of the Middle Ages in fact has its roots in a much older system of land tenure in return for military service which can be traced back to the last days of the Roman Empire. In essence feudalism was 'an institution based on the holding of a fief, usually a unit of land, in return for a stipulated honourable service, normally military, with a relationship of homage and fealty existing between the grantee and the grantor' (Holliser, *Military Organization of Norman England*, Oxford, Clarendon, 1965). Something of the kind had existed in Anglo-Saxon England, but the Normans formalized it and established a system which ensured that a ruling minority held the land and kept it by force. This created a social pyramid bound together by clearly defined rights and obligations, at the bottom of which was the serf, the peasant farmer who was little better than a slave. In developing this network of ties, the Normans created the basis of the class-system in England, which remains to this day a social fossil of the medieval past not found elsewhere in Europe, probably fuelled by the system of land 'ownership' or, more properly, tenancy (see p. 111).

Castles were the physical manifestations of Norman feudalism. They were the defended residences of the lord, and, as with feudalism itself, it has been hotly debated whether castles existed before the conquest or made their appearance as a result of it.

Land in many of the old Anglo-Saxon towns was laid waste to erect earth-and-timber motte-and-bailey castles, vivid scars on the landscape. To make room for them, one in seven wards in York was devastated, while in Lincoln 160 houses were cleared to make way for the castle. At Oxford, half the properties documented in the Domesday Book were wiped out. Other destructions, on varying scales, are recorded in Norwich, Shrewsbury, Stamford, Cambridge, Canterbury, Gloucester, Huntingdon, Wallingford, and Warwick. In at least one case (Oxford) the Normans did not even bother to clear away the houses, but built their castle mounds on top of the still-standing buildings.

In England the Normans were responsible for the construction of three types of castle – the simple ringwork, the motte-and-bailey, and the stone keep. The first two, which were of earth and timber, were built in large numbers in the years following 1066; stone keeps, which took longer to erect, were much fewer and were not put up in any number until the twelfth century.

Ringworks, as the name suggests, are simply earthworks, comprising a bank and ditch with an entrance and internal timber buildings. The bank was crowned with a palisade, and the gateway, of timber, was in some cases fairly substantial.

Mottes were more complex structures, and comprised an earth mound crowned by a timber tower. Some had one or more outer banked enclosures (baileys), and the constructional details were very varied.

In 1912 Mrs E.S. Armitage published a book on the *Early Norman Castles of the British Isles*. In it she expressed the view that the motte-and-bailey castle was introduced by the Normans from Normandy in 1066, and that such castles had been built in Normandy for half a century before the conquest. But this view has been contested. Recent research in both Normandy and England has suggested that both areas possessed a few 'castles' before 1066, but the development of the typical Norman edifices was a response to the conquest of England.

Except for some churches, building in stone was very rare in Anglo-Saxon England. At Sulgrave in Northamptonshire, however, an Anglo-Saxon earthen ringwork was built to enclose a manor house of the eleventh century, and the house here was of stone. Goltho in Lincolnshire was similarly a defended Anglo-Saxon manor, although here all the building was in earth and timber. Both these show that the idea behind castles was around before the Norman Conquest.

There are records of 'castles' in the Welsh Marches in the time of Edward the Confessor. These seem to have been the work of Norman nobles, given lands there by the king. In 1051 'aene castel' was built by 'foreigners' in the Marches, probably at Hereford, and two mottes, Ewyas Harold and Richard's Castle, situated in the Marches, may be pre-conquest, though whether the existing mottes are as early is not known. The word 'castel' was used in documents before the conquest in connection with Clavering and Dover, and it is widely believed that the erection of mottes was already taking place before the Normans' arrival.

In France, both masonry and earthwork castles were being erected in the eleventh century, although the few stone keeps, such as that of Fulk Nerra of Anjou, probably only just predated it. Earth-and-timber castles, however, had made their appearance in France as early as the tenth century, and the motte with its crowning tower may have been developed either in Normandy itself or Anjou. The addition of a bailey may have been a contribution from the Rhineland, while the idea of a ringwork and a timber gatehouse may have come from Anglo-Saxon England. Orderic Vitalis was of the view that castles were very rare in England before the Norman Conquest, and he may have been at least partly right: castles may have been the outcome of the conquest itself, and the pooling of ideas from several parts of Europe.

It cannot be emphasized too strongly what an impact the early earth-and-timber castles must have made on the populace of England. Although they are now pleasant, grassy mounds where children can play or study for school projects, when they were first erected they were vivid scars on the landscape, raw mounds of bare earth crowned by stark, timber towers. It has been inferred from clues provided by sculpture in France that some mottes at least were crowned by armoured towers, with holes through which spears were thrust to give the appearance of porcupines. In many cases the mound seems to have been as much for stabilizing the motte tower as for anything else. At one of the first mottes to have been extensively excavated, Abinger in Surrey, it was found that the tower stood on stilts deeply embedded in the mound; while at South Mimms the mound itself was so low as to be relatively unnoticeable, access to the tower being achieved through a subterranean passageway.

Mottes seem, in some cases, to have been added to pre-existing ringworks, for example at Castle Neroche, Somerset, or Aldingham, Yorks. At Castle Neroche, where excavation has brought to light some 230 northern French-style cooking pots, the motte was calculated to have taken 13,780 man-days to build – four to six months of work.

In all, about 700 mottes are known in Engand and Wales, built between 1066 and 1215. Of these, about 10 per cent are over 10 m high. Mottes both completed and being built are depicted in the Bayeux Tapestry, which shows mottes at Dinan, Rennes, and Bayeux as well as Hastings, where excavation has been carried out, but with indeterminate results.

Few stone castles were built in the eleventh century, although the Tower of London, Colchester, and Chepstow belong to this period, as do the gatehouses of Richmond Castle in Yorkshire, and Exeter. Some of the walls at Rochester and Canterbury probably belong to this period.

Essentially, Norman stone castles were rectangular keeps, with internal well and entrance at first-floor level, reached by a timber staircase protected by a stone outwork. The ground floor was a store, with a hall at first-floor level and domestic accommodation above. Most Norman stone castles belong to the twelfth century, when the Normans were well established – good examples can be seen at Rochester, Castle Rising, Goodrich, and Hereford.

William's motive in erecting the Tower of London was to overawe 'the fickleness of the vast and fierce populace' (in the words of a contemporary

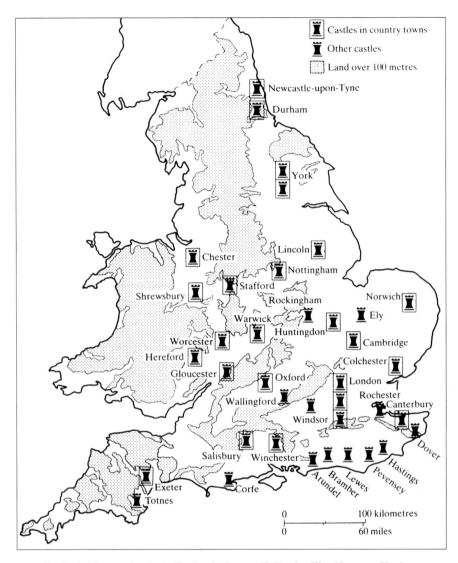

Map 8. Early Norman Castles in England. (Source: T. Rowley, The Norman Heritage, *Fig. 7.)*

historian). The Tower of London was a garrison fort, erected within a small fortified enclosure defended on one side by the Roman city wall, by the river on another, and on the two remaining sides by a ditch and probably a rampart. The castle at Exeter is thought to have been similar, erected to counteract an uprising in the south-west.

CHIVALRY AND ROMANTIC LOVE

The most enduring image of the Middle Ages is of castles, knights, tournaments, and young ladies languishing for the love of their swains. To medieval France can be ascribed the development of tournaments, jousts, chivalry, courtly manners, and the language of heraldry. The development of romantic love can be attributed to the later twelfth century, although its origins can be sought in the eleventh. It was definitely new to England. Prior to its development, in the poem *Girart de Roussillon*, the village girl was, as Christopher Hohler remarked, 'part of the furniture of any visitor's bedroom'. However, by the late twelfth century André the Chaplain in his book on love explained that peasant women really were not fair game for gentlemen, and that noble ladies should engage in polite conversation with their admirers. The emergence of romantic love was a phenomenon developed in France. Castles contained many men, fewer women. Marriage was a business arrangement, and amorous feelings would inevitably be directed outside marriage. Romantic love was the answer – it was always adulterous, but confined to faithful worship of the lady, idealizing physical passion and elevating it to an abstract devotion. Other diverse factors played their part – the elevation of the Virgin Mary in Christian belief, mystical ideas acquired from Islam during the Crusades, the writing of the Roman poet Ovid in *Ars Amoris*. From such French beginnings romantic love rapidly spread through Europe, and was introduced to England in the time of Henry II's wife, Eleanor of Aquitaine, who had previously been married to the king of France. She inspired the poetry of Bernard de Ventadour, the troubadour poet, and her daughter Marie of Champagne was partly instrumental in the composition of Chrétien de Troyes' *Lancelot*, in which the hero executed all the commands of his beloved, however unreasonable. The tradition later gave rise in England to such romantic classics as *Sir Gawayne and the Green Knight* and Malory's *Morte d'Arthur*, though by the later Middle Ages poets were having some scruples about the adulterous aspect of romance.

MONASTICISM

For those of a different temperament, monasticism held the key to contentment. Although, as has been seen, monasticism reached England with St Augustine in the late sixth century, and was established in the Celtic west even earlier, the

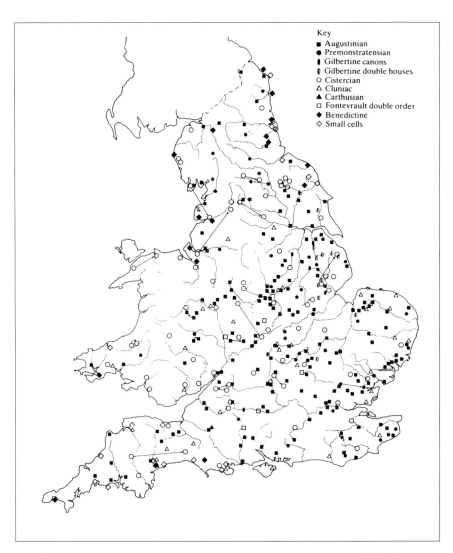

Map 9. Monasteries and houses of regular canons founded in England by 1200. (Source: T. Rowley, The Norman Heritage, *Fig. 27.)*

Golden Age of monastic expansion came with the Normans. All the major monastic orders were of Continental European origin, and the proliferation of monastic houses was actively encouraged by the Norman nobility.

The Benedictine Order was the earliest, following the Rule of St Benedict who had founded a monastery at Monte Cassino near Naples in the sixth century. The Benedictines believed that a monastery should be self-sufficient and isolated from the outside world. The Rule laid down precise instructions for everything from times of religious observance to the date at which a fire could be lit in the warming house, and although no plan was dictated for the layout of the monastery, by the ninth century certain traditions seem to have been observed.

The foundation of Benedictine houses under the Normans began with William of Normandy, who established Battle Abbey on the site of his victory, setting the high altar at the place where Harold had been killed. William brought Benedictine monks from the Continent to fill it, and from this point on until around 1200 Benedictine houses were established in England, reaching more than a thousand in number. Many of the richest monasteries of the Middle Ages were Benedictine houses founded during the first sixty years after the Norman Conquest, among them Tewkesbury, Evesham, and Malmesbury. They were richly endowed by Norman landowners and were favoured by the king. Some served as parish churches, as at Shrewsbury and Pershore, while others were elevated to cathedral status, for example Chester or Gloucester. Canterbury Cathedral itself was a Benedictine monastic church. Benedictine nunneries also existed, though these were not as common.

The Cluniac Order was extremely popular on the Continent but never took hold to the same extent in Britain. The first house was founded at Cluny in Burgundy at the beginning of the tenth century, in response to a feeling that the old Benedictine Order was in need of reform. Essentially the Cluniac monks followed Benedictine teaching, but laid increasing emphasis on liturgy and less on the ideal of manual labour.

The Pope approved the statutes of Cluny as a distinct Rule in the early eleventh century, and from 1049 the abbot of Cluny was an English monk, St Hugh. By the time of his death, 1,500 daughter houses were established in Europe. Only Cluny itself was a monastery; the daughter houses were subordinate, i.e. priories. The control exercised by Cluny made its dependencies somewhat unpopular in England, where foreign authority was regarded with suspicion, but thirty-two Cluniac priories were built, starting with Lewes, Sussex, under the patronage of William de Warenne, one of the Conqueror's strongest supporters. One English Cluniac priory,

Bermondsey, broke away from the control of Cluny in 1381 and became an abbey. The Cluniac monks were famed for their appreciation of learning, art, and architecture, and their buildings are outstanding for their architectural merit.

A third order was the Cistercian, named after Citeaux in Burgundy which was founded in 1098. The monks of Citeaux tried to return to a strict adherence to the Benedictine ideal, and pursued a simple and hard regime, as a reaction against the softening standards of traditional Benedictine and Cluniac houses. The order acquired many adherents, and was given dynamic leadership by St Bernard of Clairvaux, who died in 1153.

Cistercian houses were notably austere, situated far from areas of dense settlement, and the monks adhered closely to their vows of poverty. They were, however, exceptional farmers, famed for their skills in draining bogs and managing sheep. To this end they employed lay brethren who often lived on subsidiary granges or farms, and who were essentially labourers who farmed and lived in isolation in return for the security which membership of the monastery bestowed. They frequently outnumbered the monks – at Rievaulx in Yorkshire in the twelfth century there were 140 professed monks and between 500 and 600 lay brethren. The layout of the monastery had to be adjusted to accommodate them.

The Cistercians were, above all, the monks responsible for the development of sheep farming in England in the later Middle Ages, and they may be said to have effected an agricultural revolution which transformed the landscape of England and led to the depopulation of villages and the expansion of wealth for a few.

The first Cistercian house was founded at Waverley in Surrey in 1128; the most famous are perhaps the Yorkshire monasteries of Fountains, Kirkstall, Rievaulx, Byland, and Roche.

The Carthusians were even stricter than the Cistercians. The monks lived in individual cells and obeyed a vow of silence, only meeting for services and meals. The order is named after La Grande Chartreuse in southern France, where a monastery was built in 1084 under the leadership of St Bruno. In 1180 a Carthusian monastery was built at Witham in Somerset, but relatively few were established as the order was too strict to be popular. Among the most famous Carthusian houses is Mount Grace in Yorkshire.

Although in some respects the oldest tradition, the Augustinian form of monasticism (named after St Augustine of Hippo, an early fifth-century cleric in North Africa) did not arrive in England until the late eleventh century. Once it had gained a foothold, however, the movement spread rapidly. The Augustinians were canons; the canons regular (i.e. governed by a Rule) being based in the monasteries, the canons secular existing outside and serving as priests.

The friars, who first made their appearance in the thirteenth century, were also unenclosed, and were concerned with serving the lay community. They lived in friaries, often located on the periphery of towns, and the different types – Blackfriars, Greyfriars – were distinguished by their habits.

ROMANESQUE ARCHITECTURE

Since monasticism spread from Europe, it is hardly surprising that monastic buildings followed the contemporary architectural trends on the Continent. The style of architecture that is now termed Norman is a part of the Romanesque tradition, so termed because it derived from Roman architecture.

The Romanesque style developed first in Germany out of the tradition known as Ottonian, after the rulers. Although since the time of Charlemagne western Europe had looked to the Roman world for its inspiration, the Romanesque as a style did not evolve until the eleventh century. The first Romanesque building was perhaps the Benedictine abbey of Limburg an der Haardt in Germany, completed in 1042. The cathedrals of Trier (completed 1070) and Speyer (begun about 1030) carried on the tradition. On the Upper Rhine a two-tower façade became popular, and was taken up in Normandy in the building of Notre-Dame de Jumièges (1037–66), and in two abbeys built by William (later 'the Conqueror') at Caen, La Trinité (1062–83) and Saint-Etienne (1064–87).

Even before the conquest, the Romanesque style had caught on in England. Edward the Confessor built his abbey at Westminster (*c.* 1050–65) in the Romanesque manner, importing Norman architects for its design. It had western towers, six double bays to its nave, a transept with a crossing tower, and triple chapels with apses at the east end, although none of this has survived. Following the conquest, however, the design employed at Caen was taken up in the building of the cathedrals at Winchester (begun 1079), Ely (begun in the 1080s), Norwich (begun 1096), and Peterborough (begun 1118).

There were elements in the design of the new cathedrals that came from Germany rather than from Normandy. The sheer mass of Durham Cathedral (begun 1093) seems more directly inspired by the Rhineland churches, such as Speyer, than anything in Normandy, and Durham's rib vaulting, the earliest in Europe, seems to represent a development of German ideas. From Germany, too, came cushion and cubic capitals, fashionable on the Rhineland.

Durham, interestingly enough, was so far advanced in its vaulting that the idea was taken back to Normandy, and thence disseminated through France. In England, rib vaulting did not appear again until the twelfth century.

German influence in English Romanesque architecture can also be detected in the adoption of the 'Giant Order' – a four-storey construction probably developed out of the German westwork (a tall design for the west front of churches developed by the Carolingians). Its appearance in England has been associated with the presence in the West Country of Lotharingian clergy, for it is found both at Tewkesbury and Gloucester. Other German influences in the West Country are attributed to the same settlement of clerics.

A similar phenomenon is apparent in the West Midlands. Here the Anglo-Saxon style of church continued to flourish in Mercian heartlands for some time after the Norman Conquest. Evesham, Winchcombe, and Worcester were major Anglo-Saxon ecclesiastical centres, the last being presided over by St Wulfstan. The links between the late Anglo-Saxon Church and Ottonian Germany probably survived, and may account for the fact that clerics from Lorraine served as bishops and abbots in the area. Robert de Losinga (1079–95) built a church at Hereford modelled on Aachen – this was incorporated as a chapel in Hereford cathedral, but was destroyed in the eighteenth century. It was a square building with projecting rectangular chancel and four internal piers which carried a clerestory, a type of building common on the Rhineland, where it is known as a *Doppelkapelle.* The west front of the new cathedral at Hereford, built by Bishop Reinhelm, was also on the Rhineland model, with two eastern towers flanking the apse.

Of the purely Norman cathedrals, Winchester and Ely seem to owe a debt to the church of St Martin at Tours, though both churches also have features such as transeptal galleries linking the sides of their transepts which are to be found in Normandy churches such as those at Jumièges and Bayeux.

In the field of architectural sculpture, Norman influence seems to have made itself felt before the conquest. A typical feature of French Romanesque churches was the employment of a sculptured *tympanum* above the door of the west front. In England, there are examples, albeit crude, from Knook (Wilts) and Ipswich, though the style is much at variance with that on the Continent.

SCULPTURE AND PAINTING

Romanesque churches were adorned with sculpture and painting that conformed to Romanesque ideals. Two fine panels, now in Chichester Cathedral, depicting Mary and Martha greeting Christ at the gates of Jerusalem and the raising of Lazarus, have been the subject of considerable debate with regard to their date and the influences apparent in them. They are likely to have been taken to Chichester from the church at Selsey, and may have been part of a screen. They illustrate the mix-up of styles and attitudes after the conquest. Are they Norman or are they late Saxon? There are features about them that recall the best late Saxon work of the Winchester School, yet the figures seem to have more angular attitudes, and the draperies seem heavier and more metallic than work of the Winchester School, suggesting French comparisons. The combination of French and English elements has given rise to the suggestion that they belong to what has been termed the 'Channel style', which was current on both sides of the Channel and had its origins in links between southern England and the Continent from the middle of the eleventh century.

The Channel style is not Norman, even though it continued to flourish after the conquest. The Continental works in the style are to be found in northern France and the Low Countries, and the English counterparts on the coastal regions directly opposite them, particularly Kent and Sussex. Apart from the Chichester Reliefs, a fine ivory of the adoration of the Magi now in the British Museum is in the same style.

In addition to some other sculptures, a series of wall paintings at Clayton and Lewes priory and at Hardham (all in central Sussex), and a group of manuscripts, all display the same 'Channel style' features. On the Continent the earliest 'Channel' works were produced either by Englishmen who had settled abroad, or Continentals who had seen the English orginals. They include a manuscript probably done at Fleury, and now in Orleans, and a Psalter done at St Omer and dated AD 999. The style lingered on, its latest manifestations taking the story into the twelfth century.

Norman manuscript illuminators developed the 'historiated initial' – initial letters filled with figures or other ornament – and developed new styles in colouring and drawing. The Normans favoured brighter colours and less subtlety, and also introduced a repertoire of monsters and figures in initials, which may have originated in Bec and which were probably inspired by Eastern tapestries that were reaching the West. The Carilef Bible, executed for Bishop Carilef of Durham Cathedral between 1081 and 1096, displays the new Norman decorative trends. Carilef had been in Normandy between 1088 and 1093, and probably brought Continental manuscripts back from there – he also brought back monks to the monasteries of Monkwearmouth and Jarrow. In Carilef's Bible there is little of the old Winchester School subtlety, and in another of his books, a commentary by St Augustine on the Psalms, the firm lines and strong colours combined with gryphons suggest that, although some Winchester elements survived, here is a manuscript probably produced for English taste in a Continental scriptorium, perhaps Bayeux or Bec.

Relatively little sculpture of any note was produced in England in the years immediately following the Norman Conquest. Among those pieces that survive are some fragments from the original decorative scheme for Lewes priory, and some capitals from the crypt at Canterbury. The Canterbury capitals seem to have been carved from imported Caen stone, and a fine slab in Southover church is carved from imported Tournai marble.

GARDENS

The Normans were responsible for introducing a few of the finer things in life to Britain. The most notable of these were gardens. So far as is known, they were not in use as such in Saxon times, having died out at the end of the Roman period, although some horticulture can probably be inferred in monastic settings since there is considerable Continental evidence.

In 1064 the Normans captured Barbastro in Aragon from the Moors, and large numbers of Moorish prisoners were held in France. Some of these may have come to England following the conquest, and may have been partly responsible for innovations in English horticulture, one of which was the proliferation of vineyards. The main stimulus to gardening was, however, probably provided by the monasteries, particularly those of the Cistercians, who were responsible for the cultivation of fruit trees as well as other types of plant. At Crowland Abbey in 1091 there was an extensive fire, and records show that green trees (ashes, oaks, and willows), almost certainly deliberately planted, were destroyed. The nuns in Romsey Abbey were growing flowers before 1092, and at Barnwell Priory in Cambridgeshire (founded 1112), the refectorer was required to supply flowers, mint, and fennel.

Some of the plants cultivated by the medieval monastic gardeners have survived – when T.A. Dorrien-Smith acquired Tresco Abbey in the Scilly Isles in 1872 he found in the abbey ruins two types of daffodil growing wild, which appear to have been of North African origin. At Godstow Nunnery, Oxfordshire, birthwort, used in midwifery, can still be found growing. The most remarkable survivors of all, however, can be found on the island of Steep Holm in the Bristol Channel, where in the ruins of an Augustinian house, in use 1166–1266, can be found several medicinal herbs of southern European origin.

The historian Henry of Huntingdon (who died in 1155) wrote a study in eight books on plants, perfumes, and gems, and from the time of Henry I onwards (1100–35) royal pleasure gardens are mentioned in the records. Gardens were laid out in London associated with wells, such as the one at Clerkenwell, with trees planted along walks to provide shade.

Alexander Neckham (born 1157) compiled a number of works listing plants (*c.* 140 species), which became an encyclopedia for gardening in the later Middle Ages. Some of his plants are distinctly unusual, such as date palm, lemon, mandrake, myrtle, orange, and pomegranate, which, though exotic, appear from the context to have been grown in England. Neckham, in a prose list of plants, also mentions cedar, chickpea, cork oak, cypress, ebony, nutmeg, olive, and plane, although it is extremely unlikely that any of these were grown in medieval England.

THE NORMANS IN SCOTLAND AND WALES

The process of Normanization was extended to Wales and to Scotland. Following the harrying of the north of England, William I invaded Scotland in 1072, and, at Abernethy, King Malcolm became 'William's man' and gave over his son Duncan as hostage. The process of Normanization thus begun was, however, gradual. Alexander I (1107–24) frequented the court in England, and married a daughter of the English king, Henry I. Growing influences from Norman England, marriage alliances, and feudal relationships between the Scottish kings and the English increased Normanization in Scotland. David I spent much of his youth in England, and, like Malcolm before him, married an Anglo-Norman wife. David set about establishing Anglo-Norman institutions in Scotland, imitating the system of government that he had come to understand in the English court. He brought Anglo-Norman lords into Scotland, and soon Normans held most of the key positions in Church and State. In keeping with feudal custom, lands were settled on them. The aristocracy spoke French, and motte-and-bailey castles spread across the countryside.

In Wales the Normans established important earldoms on the borders, at Chester, Shrewsbury, and Hereford, and, under William, Gwent was colonized. However, Norman influence soon penetrated by extension from Chester and Shrewsbury, and Norman lordship was asserted in Gwynedd and Powys. William II attempted, unsuccessfully, to invade Wales three times, but following 1093 most of southern Wales was invaded and major Norman lordships were established in Cardigan, Pembroke, Brecon, and Glamorgan. In North Wales the history of English interference was prolonged and stormy.

LANGUAGE CHANGES

There were three language 'tiers' as a result of the conquest – Latin continued to be used as the 'written' language favoured by the Church and by the legal and administrative bodies, just as it had been in Anglo-Saxon England. Polite society, however, favoured French, since it was the language of the ruling élite, and French was also used commercially. English, however, remained the spoken language of the mass of the population, and the evolution of Middle English out of its Old English (i.e. Anglo-Saxon) predecessor was fairly smooth, though some French words made their impact on the English vocabulary.

A few French loan words were creeping into English before the Norman Conquest. The word 'capon', which is derived from French *capun* is one such – this was current in the writings of Aelfric. The words for 'ginger' and 'bacon' (*gingifer* and *bacun*) are also pre-conquest introductions. The conquest brought with it some suitably military words, such as *castel* (castle), *prisun* (prison), and *tur* (tower). It also provided *cancelere* (chancellor), *abbat* (abbot), *capelein* (chaplain), *curt* (court), *cuntesse* (countess), *duc* (duke), and *clerc* (learned man).

PLACENAMES

Compared with Anglo-Saxon or Scandinavian placenames in England, Norman French names are comparatively rare. Some of the names given to castles and abbeys appear to have been direct copies of names found in France, thus Grosmont Abbey was named after a mother monastery near Limoges. Some names seem to have been transferred from France because they were appropriate – Egremont in Cumbria is derived from Aigremont in France, but the name in French means 'sharp pointed hill' and there was just such a hill where the Cumbrian castle was erected.

Some Norman placenames incorporate French words such as *bel* or *beau* (beautiful). This has given us Beaulieu or Bewley ('beautiful place'), and Belvoir ('beautiful view'). Belgrave, Leicestershire, was originally called Merdregrave, and as such appears in the Domesday Book in 1086 (it means 'martens' grove'), but because it sounded to the Normans as though it came from their word *merdre*, 'filth', it was changed around 1135 to 'Bel' to make it sound more pleasant.

Some French placenames are descriptive of the terrain. Good cases can be found in Cheshire, for example Bruera ('uncultivated land covered with heather') or Malpas ('bad passage').

Very commonly, Norman scribes changed the spelling and pronunciation of existing English names, where they were unfamiliar with the sounds or combination of sounds. Thus the Normans had trouble with the *ceaster* placename element in English (pronounced 'chester'). In Norman French the 'c' was pronounced 'ts', later 's'. Thus we find Cirencester and Cerne.

PERSONAL NAMES

The Norman Conquest resulted in the appearance of a crop of new family names in England. Apart from *Normand*, meaning a Norman, we have a range of names reflecting the places of origin in France, such as Cawes (from Pays de Caux), Artiss (from Artois), Champney (from Champagne), Loring (from Lorraine), Burgoyne (from Burgundy), Blaise (from Blois), Peto (from Poitou), Gascoigne (from Gascony), Power (from Picardy), and, from outside France, Flanders and Fleming (from Flanders) and Brabazon (from Brabant, in Belgium). From the feudal families of Normandy alone are derived some 315 family names in England, with an additional further 16 from Brittany, the Somme and the Pas-de-Calais. Although some may have come in after the conquest, medieval sources contain over 240 family names of French origin still surviving in Britain today. They include names such as Dumville, Glanville, Grey, Sinclair, Lysons, Villiers, Harcourt, Lyons, Vernon, Constance, Allison, Dando, Dangerfield, Boswell, and Warren, all named after places in France.

By the twelfth century, Britain looked like an extension of France, but the ties were to be made even stronger.

CHAPTER SEVEN

The Later Middle Ages

The Normans were the last group to enter Britain under the guise of military invasion. Henceforth, influence from abroad was more subtle, and it is likely that the immigrants who arrived thus peacefully probably far outnumbered those who came via the traditional 'invasions'. As the Middle Ages progressed, Britain became increasingly caught up in European affairs, and the international scene dictated the economy of the country. War alone brought numerous job and business opportunities. Considerable effort, money, and energy were channelled into interests abroad.

The Norman Conquest put an end to England as an independent state ruled by Englishmen. Perhaps surprisingly, the only 'pure-bred' Englishman to rule since Harold has been Oliver Cromwell, and it is notable that Henry V (1413–22) was probably the first king of England to speak English habitually. As a result of such cosmopolitan rule the monarchs spent considerable energy on foreign policy and their interests abroad, and trade and internal development were notably affected. In particular, France and Scotland were caught up in English politics.

THE ENGLISH RELATIONSHIP WITH FRANCE

The Norman dynasty held sway only until 1154, when England passed from being part of a Norman empire into being part of an Angevin one. The Angevins were French; their language was Norman French, and they surrounded themselves with French people. Until the Tudors, the monarchy was very closely connected with France, a factor which had considerable effect on the population in general, even when the political arena was outside the country. Although thirty and forty years ago history teachers tended to give their pupils the impression that during the period between 1154 and 1453 Britain owned much of France, the opposite view can be seen as almost as valid from a brief overview of the fortunes of French territory.

The first Angevin king, Henry II, acquired England through his mother, Matilda, and through marriage to Eleanor of Aquitaine came to rule over Normandy, Brittany, Maine, Anjou, Touraine, Poitou, Aquitaine, and Gascony. His son Richard (the Lionheart) inherited the empire and proceeded to spend barely ten months of his ten-year rule in England, paying for this vigorous overseas policy by draining the country of money, a policy continued under his brother John. Philip II of France declared that John was a usurper, eventually invading and conquering Anjou and Normandy in 1203–4.

John's successor gave up his rights to Normandy, Anjou, and Poitou but was allowed to retain the Dukedom of Aquitaine, and thus to retain Gascony and some other territories in south-west France, but only as a vassal of the king of France.

Edward I unsuccessfully attempted to throw off French overlordship, marrying his son (later Edward III) to the French king's daughter. The subsequent bid for the French throne, in 1337, set in motion the Hundred Years War, a series of struggles that continued off and on until 1453.

Success was uneven, until the English victory at Crécy in 1346, and again, under Edward the Black Prince, at Poitiers in 1356. France became so demoralized through 'scorched earth' policies, famine, plague, a peasants' revolt, and looting by soldiers of fortune that in 1360 the Treaty of Brétigny was signed. Edward effectively abandoned his claim to the title of king of France, but in return acquired about a third of the country, as well as Calais and a hefty ransom.

The victory at Crécy was celebrated in a magnificent window in Gloucester Cathedral, a building which broke away from Continental architectural models to be the first in England in the Perpendicular style. It was during this period of hostility towards France that the English derogatory term for the French – frogs – first appeared (on account of their gastronomic preferences), and in retaliation the French called the English 'God-damns' because of their propensity for swearing.

But fortunes were to change. By 1375 the English had lost all their possessions in France except Calais, Bordeaux, and some Breton ports. The next major European episode came under Henry V, who gained almost total control of Normandy between 1417 and 1419, forming an alliance with the powerful Duke of Burgundy and marrying the daughter of Charles VI of France. By the terms of the Treaty of Troyes (1420), Henry became the heir to the French throne.

Until 1428, English control in France continued to be extended in Normandy, Maine, and Champagne, but in 1436 the English were pushed out of Paris. In 1444 a truce was signed, and Henry VI married Margaret of Anjou as a pledge of good faith. By 1453, only Calais remained in English hands.

It might be thought that all this fighting would have had a detrimental effect, but, in fact, warfare had an important role in medieval society in that it provided employment for many, distributed wealth and land through booty, and acted as a control of population.

TOWNS AND TRADE

The growth of towns and trade represented another important factor in the development of medieval society, in that by creating a rich and powerful mercantile class it enabled some to escape the rigid strait-jacket of feudal society and set the pattern for future economic development.

The growth of towns and trade went hand in hand, gradually reaching a peak in the thirteenth century. As in previous periods, Britain became part of a complex international network of trade. Although food was mostly produced at home, some areas, such as Norway, had limited resources for farming, while other places, such as the Flemish cloth-weaving cities, the wine-producing areas of France, or the major trading and administrative cities such as Venice, all had to import food to meet some or all of their needs.

England exported grain to Scandinavia, Gascony, and sometimes Italy. Bacon was exported from eastern England. Sheep were exported and imported live for breeding. English cheese was greatly sought after abroad, and Scottish salmon vied with Russian caviar in the European luxury market. England, by the fourteenth century, was producing cloth for export, while English embroideries, already well known before the conquest, continued to

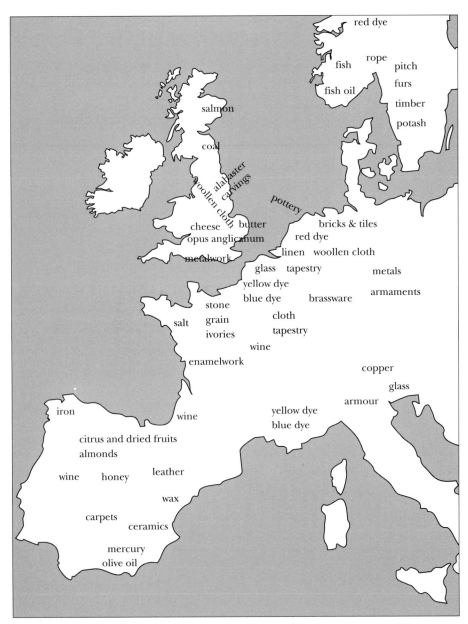

Map 10.   Medieval trade in western Europe, commodities traded. (Source for commodities: D. King, in J. Evans (ed.), The Flowering of the Middle Ages *(London, Thames & Hudson, 1966), Fig. 9, pp. 224–5.)*

be highly popular abroad. England shipped fine alabaster carvings produced in Nottingham, although in the twelfth century fonts were imported, carved out of Tournai stone. Lead and tin, both mined in England, were exported, sometimes in the form of pewter vessels. Other exports included coal, daggers, buckles, leather goods, meat, honey, and herring.

In return for this vast array of goods produced to meet European demand, imports flooded in, strongly affecting taste in Britain. Wine was of particular importance. Fleets were sailing into the Thames from the Rhineland in the twelfth century, and into Bristol in the fifteenth. Most of the wine trade, however, was derived from Bordeaux, though as time went on Mediterranean wines became more frequent imports. Initially foreign sailors brought the wine from Bayonne, but by the fourteenth century English seamen were also having a hand in the trade. In 1372 Froissart details 200 English, Welsh, and Scottish ships loading up with wine at Bordeaux. The Welsh ports either received the wine directly from the Continent, or at a second remove from Bristol. Bayonne ships are recorded at Chester by 1200, and from this point on all the Irish Sea ports seem to have engaged in the wine trade. Sweet wines were imported from the eastern Mediterranean, Syria, Cyprus, Crete, and Greece. They were collectively called *malvoicie*, malmsey, after Monemvasia in Greece. Sweet wines also came from Malaga and Tarragona in Spain, and from Italy and Sicily. In 1443–4 a year's wine imports at Southampton comprised 345 tuns (barrels) of sweet wine and 896 tuns of dry.

The list of other imports is impressive. Pitch and hemp, Swedish iron, and Ruhr steel came from the north. Despite the large areas of forest, England imported timber from the Baltic, in particular bow staves – it has been suggested that the bows used by the English at Crécy and Agincourt were fashioned out of wood from the Carpathians. Bow staves of yew also came from Spain, along with Spanish wool, used in blending as it was of inferior quality to the English. Some cotton came from the Levant, used mostly for making candle wicks in Candlewick Street, London. Dyestuffs and alum were imported for the cloth industry. Cordovan leather from Spain was much prized. Hides, fur, and oak were imported from Ireland, along with some corn, which was also sometimes brought in during times of famine from Danzig. Stock fish came from Scandinavia, salt (although

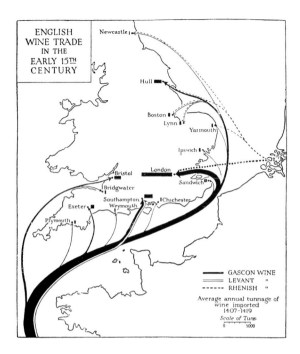

ENGLISH
WINE TRADE
IN THE
EARLY 15TH
CENTURY

Newcastle

Hull

Boston
Lynn
Yarmouth

Ipswich

Bristol
Bridgwater
Southampton
Exeter Weymouth
Plymouth

London
Sandwich
Chichester

GASCON WINE
LEVANT "
RHENISH "
Average annual tunnage of
wine imported
1407-1419
Scale of Tuns.
0   5000

*Map 11. The medieval wine
trade with England in the
early fifteenth century, based
on documentary evidence.
(Source: H.C. Darby,*
Historical Geography of
England before 1800
*(Cambridge University Press,
1936, repr. 1963), p. 323,
Fig. 62.)*

there was local production in Cheshire) from Biscay. Vegetable seeds, especially onion, were also imported. In 1420–1 London imported cloths, spices, drugs, sugar, dyes, carpets, popinjays (parrots), wormseeds, salt, woad, fur, fish, haberdashery, cabbage, oranges, raw silk, compasses, antimony, soap, and onion seed.

Cloth was imported as well as exported: cambric from Cambrai, arras tapestry from Arras (France), fustian (from the Italian *fustango*) from Italy and Flanders, and the 'fyne cloth of Ipre' (Ypres) from the Low Countries.

The luxury trade started with spices, which were mainly brought by the Genoese and Venetians. Sugar had been introduced to the Mediterranean by the Arabs, and it fetched enormous prices, particularly in northern Europe. Dates and figs, oranges, almonds, currants and raisins, olive oil and rice came from the Mediterranean. Gold and silver, jewels, silks, cloth-of-gold fabrics, damask, carpets, and glass all came from Venice. Cadiz girdles and Spanish gloves, thread from Cologne and Lyons, glass and cutlery from the Rhineland, Spanish swords, Italian armour, French bonnets: the list was endless.

Some of this trade is attested archaeologically. A skeleton of a pet barbary ape from a pit in Southampton is a reminder of the flourishing trade in exotic pets. The same pit in Cuckoo Lane, which belonged to a thirteenth-century burgess – Richard of Southwick – also produced Iranian silk, rope, and string made of palm fibres, jugs from northern France and from Saintonge, lustre ware from Spain, and a jar of Near Eastern origin. A bucket bowl came from northern Europe and some of the glass pieces came from Venice. The food remains in the pit included fig seeds, grapes, plums, cherries, raspberries, hazelnuts, and walnuts. Richard of Southwick ate well!

Finds from Hull similarly show the far-flung connections of the city. Excavations at Blackfriarsgate and Myrtongate produced a huge drip pan from Holland, olive-oil jars, and a costrel (bottle) from south-west Spain, a couple of vessels from the Saintonge area of France, a cosmetic pot from Beauvais, and a stone-glazed jug from Germany.

THE WOOL TRADE

Perhaps the most important commercial enterprise was wool. The population of England appears to have doubled between 1066 and 1300 and although more land was cultivated, and areas devastated at the conquest were repopulated, the pressure on land was considerable. It was necessary to derive as much profit from it as possible. One answer was to increase sheep farming to produce the necessary wool to supply the clothmaking cities of Flanders, and this was done, particularly under the patronage of the nobles and the Cistercian monasteries. Areas hitherto of minor economic importance, such as Derbyshire, Yorkshire, and the Welsh Marches, now assumed greater worth.

The wool trade, directed towards Flanders, was one of the most notable economic success stories of the Middle Ages. The strong counts of Flanders provided the stability for the Flemish industry to grow, and the English wool trade fed it. Wool exports were sufficient in the time of Richard I to raise the tax necessary to provide the ransom to rescue him – the proposed levy amounted to 50,000 sacks, the fleeces of 6 million sheep. Not surprisingly, English concern with wool gave rise to some well-known sayings, such as 'dyed in the wool'. To the medieval wool trade we also owe the fact that we now spin a yarn, unravel a mystery, carry on a thread of discourse, and put forward a homespun philosophy – many of these 'wool' expressions passing into modern English through Shakespeare. To this period, too, we owe the term 'spinster', and the family names of Dyer, Fuller, Taylor, Walker, Weaver, and Webster.

The peak was reached in the late thirteenth to early fourteenth century, but thereafter the trade declined. Profits remained high. At the end of the fourteenth century a sack of Cotswold wool could fetch £12–£15 in the markets of the Low Countries, and even more than that in Italy; in England it could still be sold for a profit at £4–£6 a sack. This differential enticed foreign weavers to England, and also stimulated the home weaving industry. Much of the Continental trade was in the hands of foreign merchants, but wool, backed by native cloth production, encouraged English merchants to explore new avenues. They established themselves in Scandinavia (particularly Bergen), in Danzig, and in Cologne and Antwerp. Antwerp and Bergen had full trading stations with resident representatives.

The fifteenth century saw a marked slump in the English export of wool and woollen goods, mostly due to trouble with the Hanseatic merchants (the Hanseatic League was founded in the eleventh century, new towns being established in Germany to take commercial enterprise out of the hands of Flemish and Scandinavian traders). The wool trade hit bottom in the 1460s, and though it recovered as relations with the Hanse improved, it is likely that the reduction of overseas trade had an adverse effect on the success of the home market.

Behind the growing wool trade lay financial backing, at the forefront of which were the Florentine bankers – Florence had an additional interest since it, too, required English wool for cloth production. Many Florentine bankers became involved in English economic affairs when they arrived as papal tax collectors in the time of King John. From the thirteenth century onwards they took over the role of money lenders, which had hitherto been the province of the Flemings and the Jews.

In the early Middle Ages Jews were established in most of the main towns – London, Norwich, York, Colchester, Lincoln, and Leicester all had jewries. The Crusades increased the unpopularity of Jews, and although they enjoyed some royal protection, the king did not hesitate to deprive them of any wealth they may have accumulated. Edward I expelled them when they numbered 15,000, and they did not return until the Commonwealth.

After their expulsion, the work of the Jews was carried out by Templars and Lombards. The latter, in particular, were Italian merchants, not only from Florence, but from Lucca and Sienna.

THE MEDIEVAL POTTERY TRADE

The documentation for the trade around the North Sea in the Middle Ages is considerable and has been well studied, and to the evidence can now be added a growing body of archaeological material.

Excavations in major ports have brought to light abundant evidence for the North Sea pottery trade, which, because of the modesty of the commodities involved, attracted little attention in the records. London, Bristol, Southampton, Winchester, Canterbury, King's Lynn, and Boston have all been fruitful sites, and on the Continent their counterparts have been investigated in Belgium, Holland, Denmark, Norway and Sweden (Antwerp, Hamburg, Lübeck, Kalundborg, Ribe, Bergen, Borgund, Oslo, Lund, and Ostra Tommarp). Pottery was presumably shipped as part of more varied cargoes – lustreware was imported from Spain in the late thirteenth century along with various fruits and olive oil.

Ceramic evidence shows that in the twelfth century the main category of pottery traded was red-painted ware from Badorf and Pingsdorf in the Rhineland, and its derivatives were manufactured in other parts of the Rhineland and in Holland. This ware came to the southern English ports as far west as Southampton, and extended up the east coast as far as York. Red-painted pottery was also imported in bulk from Normandy, and reached ports further afield, such as Newcastle, or Montrose in Scotland, as well as more westerly ports in England, as far afield as Devon. In the twelfth century, too, trading links were established with Bergen, where green-glazed 'developed Stamford ware' from the Midlands has been found in excavation.

The trade continued to be vigorous in the thirteenth century and later. There was a marked increase at this period in overseas trade generally,

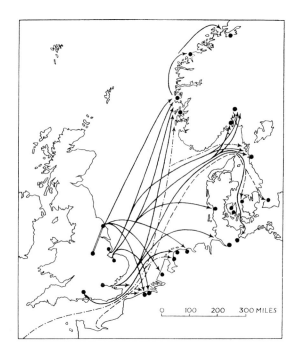

*Map 12. North Sea trade
routes (after G.C. Dunning,
in J.G.N. Renaud (ed.),
Rotterdam Papers
(Rotterdam, 1968), Fig. 31).*

particularly with France, where the Saintonge region produced green-
glazed and painted 'polychrome' jugs which were shipped in large
quantities to England, and which, by way of the Irish Sea, reached south-
west Scotland. Sherds of finely decorated jugs from Rouen and elsewhere
in Lower Normandy are relatively common in thirteenth century contexts
in England, while roulette-decorated jugs from Aardenburg in Holland
reached in particular East Anglia and even travelled as far as Dundee in
Scotland. Excavations in Dublin have brought to light quantities of pottery
from La Chapelle des Pots and other centres in the Bordeaux region,
attesting the trade in ceramics that probably accompanied the wine trade,
along with pottery from such centres as Ham Green near Bristol. Pottery
seems to have come into even relatively small ports from a great diversity of
sources – at Stonar, Kent, eight sources were recognized, four in England,
two in France and one each in the Lower Rhineland and Holland. The
pattern established in the thirteenth century continued more or less
throughout the Middle Ages, although the types and precise centres of
production varied over the years.

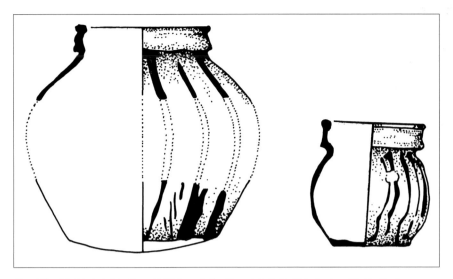

Fig. 17.   Red-painted pottery, British and Continental. Left: Winchester. Right: Paris.

The trade was not all one-way. The volume of trade from English east-coast ports was substantial, and pottery was exported from all of them to Bergen, and from most of them to Oslo and ports on the west coast of Jutland, North Germany, Friesland, Zeeland, and Flanders.

The pattern of trade represented by the distribution of Saintonge pottery in the thirteenth century is mirrored a little later in the early fifteenth century, by the well-documented wine trade with Gascony. Large quantities of Gascon wine were imported to London, and in only slightly less volume to Southampton and Bristol. Further north the wine was shipped into ports in eastern England, such as King's Lynn, Boston, Hull, and Newcastle. From southern Spain came lustreware from Malaga, which reached London, Sandwich, Southampton, and other centres in south-east England.

IMMIGRANTS

Much of England's foreign trade was in the hands of foreign merchants. For the most part these were not permanently based in the country. They were generally unpopular, as they were seen as upsetting the monopoly of

English burgesses. To control their activities, certain regulations were imposed: no foreign merchant was to remain for more than forty days in England, and had to stay with an English host who was to witnesses all transactions he carried out. The merchant was banned from retailing, and from selling to other foreign merchants. This ruling was relaxed in the case of merchants from particular cities at certain times – the Hanseatic League was one such case, in the time of Edward I. London (in 1237) and Norwich (in 1286) made separate deals with the woad merchants of Amiens which allowed them to stay in these cities as long as they pleased, and to sell their woad to whomsoever they wished.

Edward I, especially vexed at the reception given to his wife Eleanor of Castille, showed favour to foreign merchants in London. Edward III went much further, motivated by his overseas political ambitions, and in 1335 passed a statute which decreed that merchants could trade freely 'within franchise or without'. He introduced alien weavers and clockmakers, and also encouraged a group of German miners to come over and provide instruction in copper mining.

The rules governing foreign traders in England fluctuated through the Middle Ages; by the fifteenth century there were considerable numbers settled in England. Edward III suggested that they should be taxed, but it was not until 1439 that an annual tax of sixteen pence was imposed on resident aliens. By 1453 this was increased to an annual tax of forty shillings, unless they remained for six weeks or less, when they were only required to pay twenty shillings. Permanent residents were taxed ten marks.

A fear current in the Middle Ages was that money reserves would be drained out of the country, and foreign merchants were seen as instrumental in effecting this. In 1335 an act was passed forbidding the carrying of sterling out of England, and it was also enacted that 'no pilgrim pass outside our realm to foreign parts, except through Dover, under pain of a year's inprisonment'. England's supplies of gold and silver, however, were low, and money continued to be drained to the Continent. An act of 1382 forbade the export of gold and silver, and various subsequent acts tried to ensure that foreign merchants spent their money in England.

Hostility against aliens was a running theme of the medieval period. The Lombards were the victims of race riots in 1359 in London, and Flemings who said 'brod and case' instead of 'bread and cheese' lost their lives at the time of the Peasants' Revolt. The Hansards (merchants from the Hanseatic League) were protected by the defensive works they had constructed in the city. In 1456 and 1457 there were further race riots, and the Venetians, Genoese, and Florentines left London.

Flemish masons worked in England – they were employed, for example, by Bishop Poor at Salisbury, and probably in the building of Llandaff Cathedral and Caerphilly Castle. King John employed Iselbert of Saintonge as a master mason, and Edward I employed Master James of St George as master of the king's works and architect of the Edwardian castles in Wales. Master James was a Savoyard, and enjoyed a remarkably high status – in 1284 he was awarded three shillings a day for life, and one shilling and six pence for his wife, Ambrosia. He is described as an 'ingeniator', and he had come to the attention of Edward's uncle when he built a group of castles for him in the Viennois. He incorporated some features of his Savoy castle into his works in Wales, of which the crowning achievement was perhaps the concentric planning of Beaumaris on Anglesey. In less than six months in 1295 he spent £6,500 on Beaumaris alone, with official approval.

Weavers came into England from many areas. Flemish weavers were encountered at an early date at Cranbrook in Kent; others settled in East Anglia, particularly in Norwich; in the time of the Peasants' Revolt a band of men from Norwich, headed by someone from Lynn, entered Snettisham with the intention of killing any Flemings they might find. In Yarmouth they found and killed three. There are records of two weavers from Brabant setting up in York, while the appropriately named Thomas Blanket went into cloth production on a large scale in Bristol. At Castle Combe in Wiltshire Flemings started the weaving industry, but soon locals were also benefiting from it. All in all, it seems that Flemish weavers introduced craft guilds into England and pioneered capitalistic production in the time of Edward III.

Europeans were also to be found in other industries. Two to three hundred were employed by Edward I in the mint; German miners were employed by Richard of Cornwall in the late thirteenth century; Flemings are supposed to have introduced clogs and clog-making into Lancashire in the time of Edward III. In the fifteenth century, immigrants were responsible for the production of finer goods than were usually made in England. Among the most interesting are the women silk weavers of London – although they may have been English, it is more likely that they came from Italy. The idea of a guild of women was unusual for the sexist England of the time, but was not unknown on the Continent, notably in Paris.

Among the immigrants in late medieval England was John Cabot of Bristol, the leader of the first English expedition to America, who was, in fact, Genoese in origin.

LANGUAGE

Linguistic borrowings from French into English continued in the later Middle Ages. In the thirteenth century, words could be found such as mule, bar, table, feeble, charity, custom, chalice, locust, lion, feast, saint, crown, arrive, catch, fresh, striving, wait, chieftain, grant, country, mount, attire, guise, escaped, robber, nurse, prophet, saint, manciple, parishioner, adversity, prosperity, cellar, and anniversary. We also find air, desert, rock, beast, unicorn, raven, flour, fruit, balm, spice, ornament, box, journey, barren, feeble, and diet. Age, cave, heritage, envy, folly, and dragon are all found at this period. In the fourteenth century French loan-words were used all over England – many English words with the suffixes *-ance, -ence, -ant, -ent, -tion, -ity, -ment* are French borrowings from this period, as are those with the prefixes *con-, de-, dis-, en-, ex-, pre-, pro-,* and *trans-*.

By the fifteenth century no form of recreation was possible without the help of the French language, and, not surprisingly, neither was cookery. Thus we are told in a fifteenth-century cookery book to prepare *oystres* in *grauey* thus: Take *almondes*, and *blanche* hem, and grinde hem, and drawe hem thorgh a *streynour* with wyne, and with goode fressh broth into gode mylke, ad sette hit on the fire and lete *boyle*; and cast thereto *Maces*, clowes, Sugur, pouder of *Ginger*, and faire *parboyled oynons my[n]ced*; And then take faire *oystres*, and *parboile* hem togidre in faire water; And then caste hem there-to, And lete hem *boyle* togidre til they ben ynowe; ands *serue* hem forth for gode *potage*.

Many words of a technical nature passed into Middle English from French, particularly connected with law, heraldry, and arts and crafts.

COINAGE

Early in the thirteenth century English trade with the Hanse began to flourish and, in particular, from 1207 onwards, transactions were entered into with the traders of the Rhineland and the Netherlands. English short-cross pennies were used as a medium of exchange, appearing in hoards at Landenburg and elsewhere. Between 1209 and 1218 imitations of English short-cross pennies were struck at Cologne, Duisburg, and Dortmund, while English-style pennies were produced at Rhineland mints.

The key to understanding all these imitations, and, indeed, the later foreign coins that flooded Britain, is the wool trade. The varying types of copies reflect the commercial and political intrigues of the period.

The production of English-style coins on the Continent intensified in the period 1228–40, when large numbers of imitation English coins were struck in Westphalia. Trade with the Easterlings, as the Westphalian merchants were called, became so intense that it was seen as threatening the privileges of the merchants of London. After a brief intermission, the flood of English coins across to the Continent resumed by 1250. Once again they were imitated, this time on the Baltic and in Frisia. Around 1273 a massive coinage was issued in Brabant, which was technically not forgery since a crown of roses was substituted for the usual crown on the portrait of Edward I.

In 1279 Edward banned their circulation, on the spurious grounds that they were plated and of lower standard than the English prototypes. Probably as a result of this they ceased to be issued on the Continent around 1304–6.

A far bigger problem followed. Around 1310 pennies were struck on the Continent which exactly copied the English except for the legends, which were blundered. They turn up in huge numbers in English coin hoards, such as that from Boyton in Wiltshire. On occasion Scottish coins were also copied, notably at Ghent and in Lorraine. The most blatant forgeries were those struck in the time of Edward III in the Netherlands, by John the Blind of Luxembourg. In 1350 Edward passed an act which made the importing of 'Lushbournes', as they were called, punishable by death.

In the fifteenth century the Venetian fleets brought large numbers of base metal coins known as soldini, which in England were called Galeyhalpens (galley halfpence) because they had been brought in on the galleys. They were used to pay for wool. In the fifteenth century there was a notable dearth of short change in England. The imported coins were used as tokens, for many transactions could involve very small sums of money such as half a farthing. Large numbers occur as stray finds, and also turn up in hoards, for example at Highbury, London.

There were repeated attempts to stamp out the use of Galeyhalpens, but they remained an important part of the English currency for the first fifteen years or so of the fifteenth century.

Anglo-Gallic coins, struck by English kings for use on the Continent, reflect the story of medieval English territorial holdings in France. Often they are of much greater artistic merit than the English issues.

Anglo-Gallic coinage began with Henry II's marriage to Eleanor of Aquitaine, whereby he became Duke of Aquitaine. Thenceforward until the time of Henry VI, coins were struck for use in the English colonies in France. In addition, coins were struck at the mint of Calais, notably in the reign of Henry VI. These were English coins, and circulated in England as well as in France. The master of the mint in Calais was often the same person as the master of the mint in London. Henry VIII struck groats at Tournai, which were in fact English coins.

THE 'AULD ALLIANCE' – SCOTLAND AND FRANCE

One of the most enduring links in British history was that between Scotland and France – an alliance which was rarely convenient to England. The 'Auld Alliance' as it was termed, began in the thirteenth century: in 1294 Edward I was involved in mobilizing forces for the defence of Gascony, and demanded that John Baliol, the puppet king of Scotland, should provide him with military support. Somewhat surprisingly, Baliol refused, and instead signed a treaty with France in 1295. The outraged Edward marched on Scotland and the ensuing Wars of Independence resulted in Robert Bruce being recognized by England as the rightful king of Scotland. 'Good peace, final and perpetual' was declared between Scotland and England, 'saving on the part of the king of Scotland the alliance made between him and the king of France'. Despite this, Edward III had further designs on the Scottish throne, backing Edward Baliol, the son of the former king, against the rightful king David II.

In 1334 David and his queen left to take refuge in France, not to return until 1341. In the event, David was captured and subsequently ransomed by the English, who held considerable lands in southern Scotland, just as they did in France. This further united Scotland and France against the common enemy, and Robert II in 1371 renewed the alliance, as did Robert III in 1390, and James II in the mid-fifteenth century.

With the reign of James IV, Scotland became even more integrated with Europe. Suddenly the alliance with Scotland was seen as desirable among the courts of Europe since there were fears that France had grown too powerful. In 1496 the Spanish ambassador, Pedro de Ayala, came to Scotland with the express intention of switching Scottish allegiance from France to Spain. James IV was torn between the Auld Alliance and a new bond forged with England when he married Margaret Tudor. But relations with England became increasingly strained, and in 1512 the Auld Alliance was renewed, to end in James' death at the hands of the English in the battle of Flodden Field in 1513.

As a result of these political connections, Scotland was involved in importing from France, to judge by the pottery from the wine-producing areas that was reaching western Scotland in the thirteenth century. By 1596 the four-score wine ships documented in one source appear to have been mostly Scottish – claret was traditionally favoured by the Scots. Since raw materials were scarce, fine iron and leather horsegear was imported from the Low Countries. A recent find from a medieval sewer in Paisley comprised a large number of lead seals used to indicate the manufacturer and place of origin of imports. These demonstrated a vigorous import trade in cloth from the Low Countries.

GOTHIC ART AND ARCHITECTURE

Gothic art and architecture marks the highest point of medieval artistic endeavour. Gothic was a term first applied in the sixteenth and seventeenth centuries to an art that was seen to be as barbarous as that of the Goths when compared with the classicism of the Renaissance, and it was assigned loosely to anything conceived of as 'barbaric'. By the eighteenth century, when it was back in taste, it was a term applied to all medieval art, but by the nineteenth it had been segregated from the preceding Romanesque.

As far as modern art historians are concerned, Gothic began with the rebuilding by Abbot Suger of the Abbey Church of St Denis near Paris between 1122 and 1151. It has been pointed out that in the Middle Ages the spread of artistic ideas may have been in part occasioned by the travels of sightseers, sometimes on pilgrimages, the medieval equivalent of package holidays, sometimes on diplomatic missions. Already by the twelfth century people were bringing back to Britain ideas and objects from their travels – Henry of Blois, Bishop of Winchester, bought some Roman statues on a visit to the city in 1151, and sent them back to Winchester, while the Abbot of Westminster in 1269 brought back from Rome both materials and craftsmen to work them when he decided to lay down a marble pavement in Roman style in the church at Westminster.

In essence, Gothic art evolved in the Ile de France and northern France between about 1140 and 1240, and in the succeeding period spread through the rest of France and adjacent areas of Europe, including Britain.

The beginnings of Gothic in England are perhaps marked by the building of Canterbury Cathedral in 1174 and the rebuilding by Henry III of Westminster Abbey, initiated in 1245. The architect was familiar with Parisian architecture, and borrowed from it the idea of a tall clerestory with external flying buttresses. The tribune gallery has a double layer of tracery in the French manner, the plan of the east end reproduces a French layout, and the transept fronts with rose windows echoed the transepts of St Denis itself.

The essence of Gothic architecture was the use of the ribbed vault, pointed arch, flying buttress, and narrow supports to create a feeling of space. In some English buildings the French model was followed closely, as for example in the eastern part of Canterbury Cathedral; in other buildings it was blended with elements of English Romanesque, for example at Salisbury. As the later Middle Ages wore on, British Gothic architecture developed along distinctively insular lines, with the evolution of the decorated and perpendicular styles.

The Gothic style was not confined to architecture. France again provided the models for innovation in sculpture, for example in the decoration around 1170 of Rochester Cathedral with tall figures similar to those at St Denis and Chartres. Continental High Gothic reached English sculpture in the later thirteenth century; it can be seen for example in the decoration of the Angel Choir, Lincoln.

The transition between Romanesque and Gothic in painting is well exemplified by the superb Winchester Bible, a work of many hands, some Romanesque (such as the Master of the Leaping Figures), some Gothic (such as the Master of the Pierpont Morgan Leaf). French influence is apparent in Early and High Gothic work in England, but by the middle of the fourteenth century other influences were also apparent. As a result of interplay between Italy and the countries north of the Alps the International Gothic style developed, so-called because it was a European style, rather than one confined to a particular area. The Wilton diptych in the National Gallery in London is a classic example of the style, which acquired from Italy new approaches to the treatment of space.

FASHION AND TASTE

Continental fashion had already begun to influence English dress sense before the Norman Conquest – the late Saxon monk Alcuin complained that the English had forgotten their simplicity, had cut their hair, shortened their tunics, and looked to France for fashion. The Crusades indirectly also resulted in changes in fashion in England, moving in line with the Continent. Women started to assume an oriental veil, or a modification of it, the wimple. Expensive materials arrived in England, and remains of exotic fabrics have been found in York, Southampton, and Lincoln. At Southampton a piece of weft-face compound silk twill, probably originally decorated with a formal plant design, emanated in all likelihood from Byzantium, and another piece of silk from the same city was similar to that used for the turquoise blue facing of an English bishop's cloak when he was buried in 1372 in Nubia.

When Anne of Bohemia married Richard II she introduced in her retinue people from Poland (which was then a part of Bohemia), who wore very pointed shoes. These were taken up in England, and became known as crackowes (after Cracow) or poulaines (after Poland). The fashion grew more and more extreme, and lasted until around 1410. Edward III had enacted that 'No Knight under the estate of a lord, esquire or gentleman, nor any other person, shall wear any shoes or boots having spikes or points exceeding the length of two inches, under the forfeiture of forty pence'. At the time it had looked like a nice little earner for the monarchy.

On a different front, Richard II endeavoured to introduce two French customs – eating with a fork and using a handkerchief for blowing the nose – but they were accepted with less enthusiasm than they are today, the latter on grounds of lack of hygiene.

More popular in England was furniture which was strongly influenced by French design throughout the later Middle Ages, although there was also a Netherlandish influence. This was increasingly experienced in the fifteenth century, when the same taste was also being felt extensively in art, and was the outcome of the fact that Netherlands court life was becoming a model for the English. This influence continued to grow in the sixteenth century. It has to be emphasized that furniture was not merely practical in the Middle Ages; its use was tied up with status and ceremony, and the choice of particular furnishings reflected the status of the user. Degrees of honour or precedence were known as *estate*, and this governed not only use but form, ornament, and fabric. The model of Burgundy (i.e. the Netherlands) was of great importance in England on matters relating to *estate*, and it is quite clear that the English court was regarded as not inferior to that of Burgundy when it came to important matters of etiquette, as Leo of Rozmital made clear in 1465.

By the late fifteeenth century courtly manners were enjoying a last flourish. Momentous events which followed the sack of Constantinople by the Turks in 1453 resulted in the opening up of European eyes to even wider horizons. The focus of European culture was becoming Italy, and the Italian Renaissance heralded the birth of the modern world. Once again, events in Europe dictated the tempo of events in Britain.

CHAPTER EIGHT

Britain in Europe, 1500–1700

With the beginning of the Tudor age the documentation for Britain's role in Europe becomes copious, and accordingly in the space of this volume can only be discussed in the barest outline, picking out a few themes.

The Renaissance and the discovery of the New World, which marked the end of the fifteenth century and beginning of the sixteenth, were major landmarks in European history and culture. They represented a widening of perspectives. Until now trade and communication with the Orient had been overland across central Asia to the Far East, or through the Middle East. The exotic commodities such as silks and spices that the East had to offer were even more sought after in Renaissance courts, and the hunt was on for a better route to the Eastern markets. Profit was the motive of the early voyages of exploration – Henry the Navigator was concerned with paving the way for merchants who would 'never trouble themslves to go to a place where there is not a sure and certain hope of profit'. The Portuguese and Spanish led the way in exploration and conquest; Britain lagged far behind. One reason for this had been the troubles that had beset her in the fifteenth century with the Wars of the Roses. It was not until the beginning of the sixteenth century, with the rise of the Tudors and the full impact of English cloth export, that there was sufficient economic and political stability for Britain to enter the competition.

There was, however, a knock-on effect from the Spanish and Portuguese explorations. By 1520 Aztec gold and silver was pouring into Europe and in 1534 Inca wealth began filling Iberian coffers. In addition, the Spanish started working the profitable Potosi silver mines in Bolivia in 1545, and these continued to be a rich source of the metal into the seventeenth century. African gold started to come on to the market, and native European production of gold increased at Salzburg and of silver in Bohemia, Saxony, and the Tyrol. Manufacturing output could not keep up with the increase in reserves of precious metal, and the outcome was spiralling prices, not helped by debasement of the coinage. Between 1526 and 1551 the exchange value of the pound had halved and internal prices doubled. Meanwhile, the Continental reserves of precious metal overspilled into Britain. This was very bad news for those on fixed incomes, and led to serious social problems, though many of course still earned their wages in kind, and were not so affected. It also led to an increase of contact with the Continent.

IMMIGRANTS IN THE SIXTEENTH CENTURY – RELIGIOUS REFUGEES

There had been heresies and schisms in the medieval Church, but essentially everyone recognized the authority of the Pope (or, for a brief period, the Antipope). That changed when Martin Luther decided that 'monkery' was not for him, and went to teach in the University of Wittenberg, where he was disgusted by the selling of Papal Indulgences (pardons) by a monk called John Tetzel. He wrote his protests in the '95 Theses' which he nailed to the door of the parish church on All Saints' Day 1517, and thereby began the Reformation. It had not been Luther's intention to break the Church into two divisions, but that was the effect, and it gave rise to deep-rooted religious splits in sixteenth-century Europe.

Henry VIII of England used the Reformation for his own ends. Angered at the Pope's delay in the granting of his divorce from Catherine of Aragon, he ruthlessly dispensed with Papal authority. He appointed a politician, Thomas Cromwell, to look into the organization of the Church in England. This led to the dissolution of the monasteries, their lands going to the king, who sold them to merchants. In turn, they sold to sheep-farmers.

As a 'protestant' country, England was an obvious refuge for European protestants fleeing Catholic oppression. Many of these refugees came from the main industrial areas of Europe: Germany, the Low Countries, and France. They were often skilled craftsmen and women, and their skills were useful to the countries in which they found asylum.

By the late fifteenth century a considerable dislike of skilled immigrant craftsmen had built up in England – they were seen as taking work and money from the locals. In the sixteenth century there was also hostility to alien immigrants because many were destitute, and a burden on the already strained resources for providing for paupers. By the later seventeenth century attitudes had changed, but in the sixteenth century immigrants were not popular, and their movements were carefully controlled.

Although in theory encouragement ought to have been given to fellow protestants, the official line was to lay down strict immigration laws, particularly since England did not wish to incur the wrath of the countries from which the refugees came. In 1544 Henry VIII issued a proclamation ordering all French who were not denizens (permanent residents) to depart.

In some areas, however, where their skills were required, aliens were actively encouraged by officialdom. One of these was in the field of armament production. Henry VIII appointed an alien as his 'provider of instruments of war', and the post was held by immigrants through the next three reigns. Gunners and armourers came from France, Germany, and the Low Countries, and were based in Southwark and Blackfriars. Italians were also active in the industry – there was an Italian gun foundry at Salisbury Court. Norman French were employed at Pelham's Wybarn's ironworks, and on account of this were made 'denizens' in 1544.

Some industries were started as private enterprises by immigrants – silk weaving, ribbon weaving, comb making, button making, jewellery, basket weaving, and embroidery. Dutch tapestry-makers set up workshops in London, glaziers came from the Low Countries and France, printers came from Germany. Bookbinding was carried out almost entirely by immigrant workers. Felt-hat making was introduced by the Dutch and Spanish – the first hat may have been made by a hat-maker from Caen who settled in 1514.

Many monasteries were used to accommodate the immigrants – houses were built for them on the site of St Martin's in Westminster, for example. In the same way, Walloon weavers settled in the abbey at Glastonbury, under the patronage of the Duke of Somerset. They worked under an English overseer, and the materials and tools were supplied by the peer.

German exiles from Charles V were settled in the Austin Friars church in

London under a Pole. They were driven out by Mary, but some came back in the time of Elizabeth. One of the immigrants, a Mrs Dingham van der Plasse (the daughter of a Flemish knight), introduced starching to England, and offered for a fee of £5 to teach English women. As a result, she became very rich and the Elizabethan court had nicely starched ruffs.

Another foreign introduction to Elizabethan England was the use of coaches. A Fleming, William Boonen, was responsible for this, and on occasion acted as coachman to Elizabeth I.

The beginnings of the English cotton industry seem to be traceable to alien immigrants. Antwerp was the source of the first cotton imported to England, in 1560. Cotton weaving, however, did not get going in England until 1641, and production in Lancashire (in Manchester) is documented in 1660. The impetus was probably the sack of Antwerp in 1585, from which many refugees came to England, and it is notable that around this time the population of Manchester increased. In 1578 there were 10,000 people in the city; by 1635 double that number.

Engineering work was also undertaken by immigrants. The harbour at Dover saw major building works, on which Flemish workmen were employed. Among the consultants was Humphrey Bradley, a Dutch engineer, who wrote a book, *A Discourse of Humphrey Bradley, a Brabanter, concerning the Fens in Norfolk*, and who was often consulted on drainage works. Not surprisingly, other aliens were consulted regarding similar drainage works, notably in Lincolnshire. Not all were Dutch – Plumstead Marshes were drained by Giacopo Acontio of Trent, and waterworks for London were the brainchild of an Italian called Genebelli, who also worked on the defences of Gravesend at the time of the Armada.

Because it was important not to concentrate the immigrants in large ghettos, they were distributed throughout the country, and their knowledge and skill was correspondingly widely dispersed. Most towns had some immigrant population.

Different arrangements pertained to the organization and control of the immigrants in different towns. In attempting to regulate Italian incomers, Richard III had ruled in 1485 that all subsequent immigrants to England had to work for English masters. This was clearly a problem for the protestant immigrants, who were also not permitted to have foreign apprentices except their own children. In 1528 a further law was passed extending this by stipulating that no immigrant was to have a foreign apprentice or to have more than two foreign journeymen, that they were not to work apart from the English, and that their work had to be carried out in such a way that the English could learn their trade secrets. The quality of their work was also to be monitored.

The Company of Weavers seems to have had a problem – Englishmen who had learned the art of silk weaving from immigrants were setting up on their own. In the London suburbs such as Soho and Lincoln's Inn the problem was less acute, but in some of the provincial cities immigrants were banned from following trades already practised by natives – this was the case at Canterbury and Sandwich, for example.

The impact of the immigrants in sixteenth-century England was considerable. They had to provide for their own poor, and were permitted to follow their own religious observances. To further the former they set up friendly societies, from which the Trades Unions eventually developed in the eighteenth century. They also had an impact on religious thought, which led to the development of Whig ideals in the seventeenth century.

COINAGE

One attempt by an alien to introduce new technology unfortunately met with disaster. A Dutchman, Eloye Mestrell, attempted to introduce the French method of striking coins with a screw press on which he had worked in the Paris mint. The coins were called 'mill-money' because of the water mills and horse mills used to power the machinery, both for striking the coins and for rolling out the sheets of metal to the required thickness and then punching out the blanks. Around 1560 he was given rooms in the upper house of the Tower Mint, and there struck some exceedingly fine coins. But the workmen employed on striking coins by hand saw the new technology as putting them out of work. Mestrell was an easy target since he was not scrupulously honest and in 1572 he was disgraced and sacked. An attempt to restore him to office resulted in a barrage of unfair criticism of his machinery. In 1578 the old order triumphed; Mestrell was hanged for counterfeiting (of which he may have been guilty), and mill-money did not reappear in England until a Frenchman, Nicholas Briot, was employed by Charles II.

It might be noted that apart from Briot, whose coins were of exceptional merit, there were other immigrants who played a major role in the development of English coinage. The first was Jan Roettiers, from Antwerp, whose father had helped Charles II in his exile. Roettiers was made assistant to the English mint master Thomas Simon, but the two could not work together and a competition was held to see who was the better designer. Thomas Simon produced his famous Petition Crown, which had round the edge 'Thomas Simon most humbly prays your Majesty to compare this his tryall piece with the Dutch and if more truly drawn and emboss'd more gracefully order'd and more accurately engraven to releive him'. Artistically it was a masterpiece, but politics triumphed over art and Roettiers was made master of the mint, though Simon designed some of the coins.

The other designer who made a major contribution to English coinage was an Italian, Pistrucci, who was responsible for the most English of coin designs, George and the Dragon. This first appeared on the sovereign and crown issued in 1816, and is still used on modern sovereigns.

Scotland and the Continent in the sixteenth century

The fortunes of sixteenth-century Scotland were very much connected with those of France, which was now overshadowed by the might of Charles V, the Holy Roman emperor. He needed to keep cordial relations with England, as the Channel was the avenue of communication between Spain and the Low Countries. But although England was traditionally hostile to France, Henry VIII's divorce from Catherine of Aragon decreased his popularity with Charles V. France, however, still wished to maintain the 'Auld Alliance', and now England, France, and the Emperor all sought alliance with Scotland. James IV had died at Flodden, and his successor, James V, was too young to rule. The regent chosen was John, Duke of Albany, who was living in France, spoke only French and was regarded as a Frenchman. Under Albany the 'Auld Alliance' was reaffirmed in the Treaty of Rouen in 1517, and it was determined that

James V should marry a daughter of Francis I (though that did not happen for many years to come). The intrigue deepened, and Scotland was pushed one way and another by rival European factions. Matters came to a serious head in 1547 when both Henry VIII and Francis I died. The Guise family became powerful in France, and in Scotland one of their number, Mary of Guise, was the mother of the queen, Mary. The English Protector, Somerset, wanted to force a marriage alliance between Mary Queen of Scots and the English boy-king, Edward VI. His troops invaded Scotland, and defeated the Scottish army at Pinkie in 1547. Desperate, the Scots appealed to France, who agreed to help on condition that Mary was sent to France where she could be married to the Dauphin, Francis, when she came of age. It was but a matter of time before Scotland became a part of France, and it is known that three weeks before her marriage to the Dauphin, Mary signed secret papers that stated that in the event of her dying childless, Scotland would be handed over to the king of France. In the event, it did not happen, but Scotland continued to be influenced by French culture.

This cosmopolitan background led to foreign immigration, though fewer incomers are attested in Scotland than in England, but this may be because they were more readily absorbed into the populace – Scottish guilds were happy to admit Flemish artisans. Dutch printers are recorded in Edinburgh in 1582, and James VI passed an act in 1587 to allow three Flemish weavers to pursue their 'gude and godlie enterprise'. They were naturalized, permitted to become burgesses of any town of their choice, and were to bring 30 weavers and fullers and other workmen to make cloth. They had to stay for five years, and take on apprentices.

In 1600 encouragement was given to a more extensive settlement of clothworkers who settled in Edinburgh, Perth, Dundee, and Ayr. Further Flemings, tempted by the economic bribes offered by the Crown, embarked on other industries, such as saltworking, papermaking, and mining. The architecture of the Fife burgh of Culross reflects Flemish influence to a considerable degree – the pantiled roofs and the feature of windows which were glazed on the upper part and shuttered on the lower, probably owe their design to Flemish influence, although this may have been an extension of the trade with the Low Countries rather than immigration. However, Flemings did settle in Fife at this period, among them the Laings.

ENGLAND AND FRANCE

In an attempt to soften the dislike between England and France, Henry VIII met Francis I on the Field of the Cloth of Gold. The French king was not impressed with the English, asserting that 'His idea of grandeur is to put a lot of gold over everything. No taste.' In 1538–9 it looked as though there would be an invasion from France and Spain, and Henry set about constructing a major series of fortifications intended for artillery along the south coast. This was the first major coastal scheme of defence since the forts of the Saxon Shore, and money obtained through the dissolution of the monasteries was used to pay for it. Henry appointed a German master engineer, Stefan von Haschenperg, as a consultant.

The line of fortifications extended from a fort at Tilbury to defend the Thames estuary round the coast of Kent, with forts at Sandown, Deal, Walmer, Sandgate, and Camber. Further west, the Solent was protected by Hurst Castle. Southampton Water was served by Calshot Castle and Netley Castle, and there were blockhouses at East and West Cowes. From there the line of forts continued south to Cornwall, to Falmouth and Dartmouth. Unlike earlier castles, they were specifically designed for artillery warfare, with a concentric plan and with bastions and parapets to deflect cannon fire. In the event they were never needed, and remained the most expensive and extensive scheme undertaken until this century. Despite the averted invasion, relations between England and France remained strained. In the seventeenth century Voltaire returned from a visit to England pronouncing 'Imagine a country with 350 religions and only one sauce!'

OVERSEAS TRADE IN THE SIXTEENTH CENTURY

The sixteenth century was a period in which the cloth trade thrived. Lead, tin, leather, butter, cheese, and also, on occasions, corn were all exported as well, but the cloth export made up about 80 or 90 per cent of the total. London boomed as a port, particularly for the export of cloth to Antwerp.

Trade generally declined in the later part of the century, particularly that with Antwerp, with resultant social problems and unemployment.

At the centre of trade was the Merchant Adventurers, a trading consortium that won the support of the Crown, which stood to benefit from its activities. The Hanseatic rights were withdrawn in the reign of Elizabeth, and in 1564 the Merchant Adventurers were given a monopoly of trade from the Baltic to the Somme, and a free licence to export cloth. Increasingly they moved further afield seeking markets, and came into conflict with the Hanseatic League. In 1597 the Merchant Adventurers were expelled from Stade. As a result of this, most English trade in the late sixteenth century was conducted by Englishmen, and the export of cloths from London by foreign merchants dropped between 1540 and 1610 from 60,000 cloths to a mere 5,000.

One of the outcomes of this decline was the quest for new markets in the East, spearheaded by the East India Company. This exported bullion and, to some degree, lead, tin, and cloth, importing the traditional merchandise of the East, silk and spices as well as indigo, calico, and saltpetre. Barely established, it came into conflict with Portuguese and Dutch interests. In the next century Cromwell negotiated a treaty with Portugal (in 1654) for freedom of trade, following the first Dutch War.

One of the main categories of exports were the 'new draperies' which were lighter than the old cloth. London and the Merchant Adventurers traded in cloth with the Low Countries and Germany, while long-distance trade was in the control of Newcastle, Hull, and York, among other centres, these places exporting heavier cloths from Yorkshire to the Baltic. Ports in the south-west, Weymouth, Plymouth, and Exeter, exported cloth to France and Spain. Unfinished cloth was sent abroad, where it was finished in Holland, Flanders, and Germany.

GLASS

English glassmaking began in the Middle Ages, with the arrival of families from Normandy and Lorraine who set up in the forests of Surrey, Sussex, and Kent (a copious supply of wood was necessary for fuel), then subsequently moved to Gloucestershire and elsewhere. In the fourteenth century John le Alemayne (a German) was producing window glass and 'fine cuppis to drink', and the Scurterres were a famous glassmaking family in the same century, as were the immigrant Peytowes in the fifteenth, but it was not until the sixteenth century that glassmaking became a major industry in England, as English glasshouses could not compete with the fine tableware from Venice.

The impetus for Tudor glassmaking came indirectly from Lorraine, through the activities of Jean Carré, who came from Antwerp around 1567 and had obtained a licence to produce window glass by the Lorraine method. Carré did not stop at window glass, however, and moved into the field of cristallo glass production '*à la façon de Venise*'. This 'Venetian' glass was produced at Crutched Friars Hall, where Carré had working for him one of the master glassmakers from Venice, Jacopo Verzelini. After Carré's death, Verzelini went on producing Venetian cristallo glass and was given a patent by Elizabeth I in 1574 to manufacture Venice glass for 21 years. Some of his products have survived. Glass monopolies were jealously guarded and fought over during the later sixteenth and early seventeenth century, but a temporary setback which banned the use of wood for fuel (in the 'Proclamation Touching Glasses' in 1615) led to the development in England of crystal glass, produced on Tyneside. At this time George Ravenscroft (1618–81) developed flint (i.e. lead) glass, which despite initial difficulties was perfected by 1676. His finest works bore the raven's head seal (it is still the badge of the Ravenshead Company). By the end of the century England was at the forefront of glass production in Europe, and remained so through the eighteenth century, until early nineteenth-century taxes forced some leading English glassmakers to move to Ireland, where they set up at Waterford and elsewhere and brought Irish glass to prominence in the European market.

POTTERY

The sixteenth century also saw continuing imports of pottery to Britain. At the end of the fifteenth century French green-glazed pottery, particularly 'chafing dishes', and pear-shaped bottles with suspension loops known as 'costrels' carried on the tradition of earlier medieval trade in French ceramics. These imports, and others from Germany, probably inspired the native Tudor green-glazed relief-moulded wares, with Tudor arms, Tudor roses and other designs, which are often so close to the Continental products that they have been mistaken for them. A clear buff glaze, in imitation of the German, also became fashionable in Tudor England.

In the late fifteenth and sixteenth centuries tin-enamelled pottery became fashionable, first in Italy and then in France and the Low Countries. This ware, known as maiolica, was brightly painted, often with complex pictures. By the time maiolica was becoming fashionable in England, however, it was already going out of fashion in Italy. The immediate inspiration for the English products did not come from the finer Italian dishes but from the derivative products of the Netherlands. The first manufacturers in England may have been Jasper Andries and Jacob Janson, who are recorded as in operation in Norwich in 1567 but who had moved to London by 1570. They are described as coming from Antwerp, but Jasper Andries appears to have been a relative of the Italian Guido Andries, who founded the Netherlandish maiolica industry.

The sixteenth century saw a marked increase in the import of stonewares from the Rhineland – these mostly comprised jugs with mottled surfaces known as 'tiger ware', which were much prized. The technique of production was similar to that of maiolica, and the products were sometimes overpainted, mostly in blue. Copies were made in England with metal mounts, and again there has been some dispute as to whether they were produced in England or on the Continent. Some are dated, the earliest being of 1549–50, and they continued in production into the seventeenth century.

Tin-glazed 'maiolica' was produced on the south bank of the Thames early in the seventeenth century, notably at Lambeth and Southwark. The earliest products were in Italian–Dutch style, and a dish closely following Antwerp design is dated 1600. Adam and Eve and the Tree of Knowledge became a popular subject for the makers of English maiolica, the earliest versions of which appear to be very close to their Italian models. Such 'chargers' became highly prized by the rich of seventeenth-century England, and were the equivalent of the imported Italian maiolica used to decorate chimney pieces or sideboards.

FASHION

Changing Continental influence mirrored political events in the field of fashion. The sixteenth century saw a modification of the medieval styles, and opened with a fashion derived from Germany. This was not peculiar to Britain, but reached England through a series of marriage alliances – the Guise family, who were half German, were influential in the French court, and probably brought about the widespread adoption in France of a style originally copied by German mercenaries from Swiss troops. When Henry VII's sister Mary married Louis XII of France, the fashion crossed the Channel.

Typical of these early Tudor clothes were shoes with very broad toes, and copious slashing. Hose were sometimes worn in the German manner, with one leg yellow, the other black, slashed with taffeta. The Schaube – an overcoat shaped like a cassock – was also a popular innovation from the Continent. It was the mark of the scholar (Thomas Cranmer wore one), and is frequently seen in Holbein portraits. Red, again very popular in Germany, became the hot fashion colour.

In the middle of the sixteenth century Spanish taste took over. In contrast to the copious material of the earlier sixteenth century, clothes were now close fitting, and the fashionable colour was black. Charles V was the first to adopt it; Henry III of France followed suit. When Mary Tudor married the Spanish king, Philip, the Spanish style became all the rage. Spain continued to influence fashion into the 1600s, but increasingly other regions contributed to the changing taste.

Around 1580, the French farthingale was made popular, perhaps through being worn by Elizabeth I. There was also an Italian farthingale made of wire. From around 1570 breeches became known as venetians – the baggy varieties were 'gascoynes'. At this period Spain contributed boots of Cordovan leather, and fine gloves.

The Cavaliers were the snappy dressers of the time of Charles I. Their extravagant clothes were inspired by fashions in France. After an intermission during the time of the Commonwealth marked by austerity in fashion as in everything else, France inspired the clothing of Charles II and his court at the Restoration. At the end of the seventeenth century the Persian mode reached Britain, again from France, and marks the beginning of modern trends.

ENGLAND AND HOLLAND

During the sixteenth and seventeenth centuries there was a considerable amount of contact between England and Holland. England was ruled for a while by Dutch monarchs, William and Mary of Orange, and in the years preceding this there had been a period in which Dutch ideas, customs, and values were extensively assimilated. Some contact was occasioned by immigrations in the wake of the religious persecutions, but there was also vigorous trade and the borrowing of ideas by Englishmen who went to Holland. In the late seventeenth century, wrote Cunningham, 'we have not a few cases of Englishmen who visited Holland for a time, and became familiarized with Dutch political, industrial, or commercial practice; it would be almost true to say that there was hardly a leading man in the last half of the century, from Charles II downwards, who had not some experience of the kind' (W. Cunningham, *Alien Immigrants to England*, London, George Allen and Unwin, 1897, 193–4).

A feature of early seventeenth-century trade had been the flourishing of companies that effectively exerted a monopoly – the Merchant Adventurers and East India Company are two major examples, the Turkey Company is another. Growing fears of the success of Dutch and other alien merchants led to the Navigation Act of 1651 which was intended to oust the Dutch from English trade. A proposed bill for the general naturalization of aliens was met with enormous hostility in London, as it was feared that, if naturalized, the foreigners would become rich and take the money out of the country, and that the products manufactured by the immigrants would damage the sale of English goods.

After 1610, however, aliens had been permitted to be shareholders in the East India Company, and as the century progressed the power of the companies weakened. It has been pointed out that company trading was a British institution, not found in France, Holland, or Portugal, although France and Holland had state-controlled companies which were, in effect, departments of state. Banking became increasingly important, and among the bankers were Dutch and French who were very influential, with Puritan and Whig sympathies.

Some of these rich men were responsible for major enterprises. One such was Cornelius Vermuyden, who was concerned with reclamation in the east of England of what he described as 'a continent of 400,000 acres'. Hatfield Chase was another area prone to flooding and suitable for reclamation, extending to some 70,000 acres. The draining of Hatfield Chase was begun in 1628, when Vermuyden was allowed to keep a third of the land he succeeded in reclaiming. Dutch financiers in London, Amsterdam, and Dordrecht put up the capital, and skilled men were brought over from Holland to carry it out, to the disgust of the locals. Riots ensued. Eventually the Dutchman sold out to a Frenchman, who introduced French workers from Normandy and Picardy to carry on – riots were unabated, and in 1650–1 some eighty-two houses were damaged and the church of Sandtoft partly destroyed.

Dutch influence was also responsible for improvements to dyeing, notably by Kepler at Bow in 1643 and by Bauer (a Fleming) in 1667.

Clocks made in England had been of French design, and Frenchmen had been introduced to make the clock for Henry VIII at Nonsuch Palace. French names are notable in a 1622 list of clockmakers. However, Dutch clocks replaced them in the later seventeenth century, the beginning of the industry being attributed to Fromantil.

Dutch miners operated at Keswick in the Lake District, and gunpowder to blast rock was introduced by German miners who had been brought by Prince Rupert to work at Ecton, Staffordshire. Here the potteries were boosted by the Dutch, who introduced salt-glazing from Amsterdam, copying Saxony ware near Burslem. Around the turn of the century they set up potteries at Chelsea, Vauxhall, Fulham, Battersea, and Lambeth which produced the famous 'Delft' blue-and-white ceramics, of which Lambeth Delft is perhaps the most famous.

The art of sugar refinement originated with the Germans in the seventeenth century. Another skill was brewing which, although native, was improved upon by the Dutch and Germans. The former operated breweries in London in the time of James I. In the early seventeenth century root crops were introduced from Brabant and tastes in ornamental gardening came from Holland.

In the seventeenth century the Dutch were the main commercial nation of Europe. They controlled the herring fishery and trade, and were the main transporters. Amsterdam doubled as a trading centre and a commercial hub. The Dutch built better ships than the French or English; they accumulated capital, had low interest rates, and were able to invest their resources into profitable ventures. The English looked on the Dutch with mixed feelings.

EUROPEAN INFLUENCE IN ENGLISH ART

The Tudor age began with the growing awareness of the artistic developments that the Renaissance had brought. The first real impact of the Renaissance in painting came with the arrival of Hans Holbein the Younger, a German by birth who lived in England between 1527 and 1529 and again from 1531 to 1543. Through his influence English art was made familiar with Classical tradition, with perspective, and with illusionistic effects. His most notable contribution was in the field of portraiture, which was also the forte of Hans Eworth, a Flemish exile who was operating in the middle years of the century. An immigrant was similarly responsible for the major sculpture of the early sixteenth century – Pietro Torrigiano, who produced realistic tomb effigies for Henry VII, his wife Elizabeth, and his mother Margaret Beaufort, as well as working in the early years of the reign of Henry VIII.

Architecture in the early sixteenth century was also influenced by Continental trends – classicism, derived from France, dictated the design of Nonsuch Palace (Surrey), and French classicism remained a dominant trend into the time of Elizabeth. A more extravagant form of classicism came from Antwerp in the time of Elizabeth I, and can be seen in Burghley House, built in the 1560s.

Prior to Cromwell the seventeenth century was a period of magnificence in the arts in England. The rich were keen collectors, and none were as avid as Charles I, whose collection, had it survived intact, would probably be the greatest assemblage of Renaissance art in Europe. Charles owned the Mantegna cartoons (which were at Hampton Court), Leonardo da Vinci's sketchbooks (which are still at Windsor), the Raphael cartoons (now in the Victoria and Albert Museum), and the Wilton diptych, newly restored and on display in the National Gallery. Through his patronage, Rubens and Van Dyck, both Dutch artists, came to England. Van Dyck's portraits were an inspiration to English artists and gave new life to the tradition that had flourished in Tudor times; immigrant sculptors, le Sueur (French) and Fanelli (Italian) revitalized the previously moribund traditions of English sculpture, although they were not in the same league as the two great painters.

Van Dyck was not the only foreign painter to play a major role in the development of English art. Sir Peter Lely (1618–80) and Sir Godfrey Kneller (1646–1723) were both immigrants. Lely was the leading light of Restoration art, after the accession of Charles II. He too was Dutch. Kneller, who came from Lübeck, was a copious portraitist, and his style was copied widely.

Britain produced her own architects of note in the seventeenth century, such as Inigo Jones and Christopher Wren, but Jones was inspired by Classical architecture and trends in Italy, particularly the work of Palladio in the sixteenth century. The Continental baroque style took a time to gain favour in England, but did so with the Restoration.

As the eighteenth century dawned, taste was coloured by growing awareness of the Classical treasures of the Mediterranean, many of which had been seen and a few of which had been brought back by travellers on the 'grand tour'.

HOMES AND GARDENS

English interiors in the sixteenth century reflected European trends. Henry VIII encouraged Italian craftsmen to set up in England, and through their influence, ideas of ornament, including medallion heads carved on furniture (Romayne work), gained widespread acceptance, often juxtaposed with a native ornament of Tudor roses, linenfold panelling, and Gothic detail. Many cabinetmakers of Dutch or Flemish origin settled in England, and produced furniture for the English market. The inventory compiled in 1542 for The Vyne, a fine house in Hampshire, lists nineteen seats, seven of which were imported and described as 'Flanders chairs'. Other chairs popular at this time were light and designed for bedrooms, based on the French *caquetoire*.

In Elizabethan England the growing links with Germany and the

Netherlands led to pattern books arriving in Britain with designs for furniture and architecture. Several elements made their appearance as a result – strapwork, low-relief arabesque carved ornament, bulbs on legs, and marquetry in floral and rectilinear patterns, executed in such materials as bog oak, sycamore, walnut, ebony, holly, and box.

During the seventeenth century, prior to the Restoration, English furniture did not mirror Continental taste, but in the later seventeenth century baroque Italian style reached England by way of France and Holland. France in the time of Charles II was the arbiter of good taste, and Louis XIV had set the pace by establishing in his court some of the best craftsmen of his day. In 1663 a pamphlet was published entitled *England's Interest and Improvement*, in which it was stated that the French 'had introduced new modes and new tastes and set us all agog, and having increased among us considerable trades, witness the vast multitude of broad and narrow silk weavers, makers of looking glasses, paper, fringes and gilded leather'.

To this French influence may be added that from the Low Countries. Following the Revocation of the Edict of Nantes, the large number of Huguenot immigrants included several highly talented craftsmen, pressed into the service of the king: Richard Vanhuissen, Peter Pavie, and Cornelius Gole, to name but three. This led to a strong Dutch influence over taste in Court (further strengthened by the residence of the Stuart court for a while in Holland). A further influence was provided by Portugal, as Catherine of Braganza, the Portuguese queen of Charles II, probably brought furniture with her. Among the skills introduced by the Huguenots was veneering on a wooden base. Among the influential craftsmen was André-Charles Boulle, who operated from Paris and in whose studio served William III's architect, Daniel Marot, whose influential designs were published in 1702.

The 'Golden Age' of English gardens was perhaps the eighteenth century, but the foundations of garden design were firmly laid in the seventeenth, under European stimulus. From the Italians English gardeners learnt of the uses of water, and the delights of intricate layouts. From France, they acquired a taste for the grand, and for wide open spaces. From the Dutch, they took ideas about shrubs, trees, and flowerbed design.

The immediate inspiration for the gardens of English country houses in the seventeenth century were Louis XVI's sumptuous gardens at his palace at Versailles. They inspired local versions in West Germany, Denmark, Holland, Italy, and Russia, in England (Hampton Court and Melbourne), and in Ireland (Kilruddery).

The accession of William and Mary introduced important gardening ideas from the Low Countries, most notably a taste for topiary, clipped trees, and statuary, although the latter had been an important feature of Italian Renaissance gardens as well. Among the admirers of Italianate gardens was the diarist John Evelyn.

Throughout the seventeenth century the lifestyles of the rich in Britain reflected Continental taste, which was international rather than regional, and progressively the volume of evidence for European and other influences increases. From then on, emphasizing Britain's uniqueness and separateness from her neighbours must have been a formidable intellectual challenge.

LANGUAGE BORROWINGS

Such extensive overseas contact considerably extended the English vocabulary. French borrowings are numerous. Some came from wine making, such as spigot and rack, while the colloquial word 'lingo' first appears in English in 1660. Troubadour, which is usually associated with medieval minstrels, does not appear until 1727, charade in 1776, chalet in 1816. Among other borrowings, mention may be made of serviette (late fifteenth century), trophy (1513), pioneer (1523), pilot (1530), cartridge (1576), rendezvous (1591), gauze (1561), partisan (1555), scene (1540), machine (1549), table d'hôte (1617), mêlée (1648), ballet (1667), unique (1602), soup (1653), nonchalance (1678), and tête-à-tête (1697). Connoisseurs were first encountered in 1714, while English people first found themselves in a cul-de-sac in 1738.

Low German words (Dutch, Flemish, and Continental Saxon) make up an important element in English. It is to this source the British owed the poll tax and the predilection for booze. Most of the borrowings came in during the sixteenth century, though quite a number are medieval. Of commoner borrowings, mention may be made of bounce, mart, wainscot, spool, pickle, deck, buoy, hoist, bulwark, boor, loiter, dock, uproar, wagon, hawker, flue, groove, manikin, mum, domineer, frolic, brandy, duffel, smuggle, easel, stipple, decoy, morass, shamble, and snort.

Italian has contributed much to English. Many Italian words came through French, and most borrowings belong to the sixteenth century and later. Traffic, race, and umbrella are Italian. Florin, artisan, gambol, panache, pistol, carnival, scope, garb, concert, rocket, citadel, bandit, cavalcade, porcelain, settee, ferret, pedestal, cornice, piazza, cameo, lagoon, balloon, cascade, corridor, ditto, gusto, vista, piano, replica, studio, figurine, and inferno are also derived from the language.

Spanish words passed into English by way of French, but also came directly from the sixteenth century onwards, largely through Spanish trade. Cask, sherry, rusk, renegade, booby, comrade, galleon, cannibal, negro, mosquito, banana, cargo, embargo, cockroach, and turtle tell their own story of travel and trade.

Portuguese has given marmalade, mandarin, madeira, molasses, palaver, and massage.

Postscript

From the time of the Act of Union with Scotland (1707) British feelings of separateness from Europe considerably increased. From the early eighteenth century onwards the emphasis was on Britain's uniqueness, on its unified and strong position and on British influence on the rest of the world rather than vice versa. Warfare on and with the Continent (especially the war with France between 1793 and 1815) certainly helped to foster this attitude and relations with Europe became increasingly complex.

The study is further complicated by the vast increase in influence from areas outside Europe – India, China, Africa, and the New World. The relationship with Europe changed subtly, but was nevertheless significant. Britain still depended on its European trade, and cultural influences from the Continent remained significant.

The complexity and copiousness of the evidence for the last two centuries makes any attempt to summarize it facile. In one area of life – language – the extent of continuing European influence perhaps epitomizes the trend as whole. The loan-words taken from European languages (as well as from others as far afield as Tibet) are a clear indication of close contacts and themselves indicate the areas in which influence prevailed.

Given the strong Germanic element in the royal family it is perhaps surprising that fewer Germanic influences have filtered into the language. More than half the eighteenth-century contributions were mineralogical or geological rather than cultural – cobalt (1728) or shale (1747), for example. In 1756 pumpernickel made its appearance and a zigzag arrived in 1712, some sixty-two years before an iceberg. Poodle arrived in 1825 and lager in 1853, to be followed by protein in 1869 and rucksack in 1895.

From the nineteenth century Scandinavia has given English the words vole, ski (1885), marram grass, fiord, and saga (1709).

The early and late eighteenth century brought in a large number of words from French, many connected with the French Revolution (emigré – 1792, guillotine – 1793, regime – 1789). Although these and military words such as ricochet (1769) and espionage (1793) might be expected, a large number of words relate to the more peaceful side of life.

The French enhanced the English language with clique (1711), savant (1719), envelope (1707), salon (1715), bouquet (1716), bureau (1720), canteen (1737), and croupier (1707). They brought précis (1760), brochure (1765), and avalanche (1789). In 1748 the English were introduced to the pompom, in 1727 to a toupée and in 1706 to ramekins, rissoles, and casseroles. Liqueur was added in 1742. Brunettes (1712) could go on picnics (1748) unless etiquette (1750) or a migraine (1777) forced them to go to a fête (1754) instead.

The nineteenth century introduced more French words into English than at any time since Middle English, mostly in art, literature, and dress. The English may not have liked the French as immigrants but they admired their culture and way of life. Bezique (1861), lacrosse (1867), crèche (1882), abattoir (1840), clientele (1860), and parquet (1816) were introduced along with such modern essentials as crêpe (1825), blouse (1828), decolleté (1831), trousseau (1833), lingerie, and negligé (both 1835). Svelte (1817) gourmets (1820) frequented restaurants after 1827 where they might partake of soufflés (1813), sorbets (1865), and mousses (1892). If it were after 1884 or 1890 respectively they might be dressed in suede or chiffon. After 1802 they might be kept under surveillance.

Italian loan-words began to arrive directly in the eighteenth and nineteenth centuries rather than through French, and relate mostly to art, music, and literature.

Thus came soprano (1730), maestro (1797), cantata (1724), concerto (1730), portfolio (1722), picturesque (1703), and dilettante (1733). One might, after 1753, visit a casino, or (after 1797) eat semolina, a cantaloup (1839) or gelatine (1800). An extravaganza arrived in 1789, viva! in 1700, a fracas in 1727, a vendetta in 1855, and a firm (as in trading company) in 1744.

Spanish words are less common, though stevedore (1788), quadrille (1738), marinade (1704), caramel (1725), carmine (1712), and cigar

(1735) have endured. Both Spanish and Portuguese words came in mostly after 1600 when Elizabeth granted the Charter to the East India Company. Many exotic words thus came in via the trading company through the two languages. Through Portuguese from the East came pagoda (1653), tank (1616), and caste (1613). From Africa came palaver (1735) and from India veranda (1711).

The story of British relations with foreigners in the nineteenth century changes focus from relations with other Europeans to relations with other races. From this time on, but increasingly in the late twentieth century, the question of race became important.

There have, of course, been numerous other influences from the Continent in the past three hundred years, but it lies outside the scope and size of this book to discuss them. Both world wars saw an influx of refugees and prisoners of war who often remained to settle. The German archaeologist Gerhard Bersu for example was, while a prisoner of war, permitted by the Manx authorities to excavate ancient sites on Man where he remained for the rest of his life.

The ease with which the population may currently move between European countries has probably never been equalled since the Roman period.

The previous chapters have outlined the manner in which the character of British culture was formed or modified through European influence from the earliest times. So fundamental was this influence that the complexity of Britain's relations with the rest of the world over the past three centuries may obscure but cannot obliterate that heritage. A small cluster of islands on the edge of the European landmass, Britain has never been able to exist in isolation, and its cherished differences from its Continental neighbours are as much a result of their agency as an assertion of their separateness from them.

Further Reading

No single book covers the same ground as this one, and interested readers should begin by consulting some of the key period surveys in which Britain's links with the Continent are discussed in their wider context. In the bibliography that follows only books are listed, although there is a considerable body of periodic literature containing key studies which have been consulted in the writing of this book. Particularly useful articles can be found in *Proceedings of the Prehistoric Society, Britannia,* and *Medieval Archaeology*. Useful information is also to be found in *Current Archaeology*, which reports recent discoveries in Britain. Most of the books listed below have extensive bibliographies.

PREHISTORY

For British prehistory the best surveys are those of T. Darvill, *Prehistoric Britain*, 2nd edn, London, Batsford, 1987; and the more detailed but also more technical J.V.S. Megaw and D.D.A. Simpson (eds), *Introduction to British Prehistory*, Leicester, Leicester University Press, 1979. For the Early Iron Age, B.W. Cunliffe, *Iron Age Communities of the British Isles*, 3rd edn, London, Routledge, 1991, is the standard account. Among other publications, mention may be made of D.W. Harding, *The Iron Age in Lowland Britain*, London, Routledge & Kegan Paul, 1974; and for coinage R.D. van Arsdell, *Celtic Coinage of Britain*, London, Spink, 1989. A useful and relevant collection of articles can be found in S. Macready and F.H. Thompson (eds), *Cross-Channel Trade between Gaul and Britain in the Pre-Roman Iron Age*, London, Society of Antiquaries, 1984. Although now somewhat out of date, E.G. Bowen, *Britain and the Western Seaways*, London, Thames & Hudson, 1971, has some interesting observations on sea routes, not just in prehistory. Similarly wide chronologically, but much more up to date and scholarly is S. McGrail (ed.), *Maritime Celts, Frisians and Saxons*, London, Council for British Archaeology Research Report no. 71, 1990, which is a collection of papers on boats and seaways. The classic study of geographical factors affecting Britain's early history was C. Fox, *Personality of Britain*, Cardiff, National Museum of Wales, first published in 1932 but with many later editions.

ROMAN PERIOD

The literature on Roman Britain is overwhelming in its quantity. The classic accounts are P. Salway, *Roman Britain*, Oxford, Oxford University Press, 1981; and S.S. Frere, *Britannia*, London, Routledge & Kegan Paul, rev. edn, 1978. Useful shorter surveys in paperback are M. Todd, *Roman Britain 55 BC–AD 400*, London, Fontana, 1981; and J. Wacher, *Roman Britain*, London, Dent, 1978. The study of Romanization began with F. Haverfield, *The Romanization of Roman Britain* (4th edn, rev. G. Macdonald), Oxford, Oxford University Press, 1923, which is still worth reading. More recent is H.H. Scullard, *Britain, Outpost of Empire*, London, Thames & Hudson, 1971; B.C. Burnham and H.B. Johnson (eds), *Invasion and Response: the case of Roman Britain*, Oxford, British Archaeological Reports 73, 1979; and more recent still is M. Millett, *The Romanization of Britain*, Cambridge, Cambridge University Press, 1990. On specific topics, S. Ireland, *Roman Britain: a Sourcebook*, London, Croom Helm, 1986, and A.R. Burn, *The Romans in Britain*, Oxford, Blackwell, 1969, are useful for documentary sources and inscriptions; and A.K. Bowman, *Life and Letters on the Roman Frontier*, London, British Museum Publications, 1994, is a fascinating account of the Vindolanda documents. B. Cunliffe, *Roman Bath Discovered*, rev. edn, London, Routledge & Kegan Paul, 1984, is interesting for its account of the population in one spa town. Art is dealt with comprehensively in J.M.C. Toynbee, *Art in Roman Britain*, London, Phaidon, 1963, and her *Art in Britain under the Romans*, Oxford, Oxford University Press, 1964. The Romanization of Celtic cults is dealt with in M. Green, *The Gods of the Celts*, Gloucester, Alan Sutton, 1986; and in A. Ross, *Pagan Celtic Britain*, London, Routledge & Kegan Paul, 1967. Other cults in Roman Britain are summarized in M. Green, *The Gods of Roman Britain*, Aylesbury, Shire, 1983; and E. Harris and J. Harris, *The Oriental Cults in Roman Britain*,

New York, E.J. Brill, 1963. Imports can be found in passing in G. de la Bedoyère, *The Small Finds of Roman Britain,* London, Batsford, 1989; while the pottery trade is dealt with in D.P.S. Peacock, *Pottery in the Roman World,* Harlow, Longman, 1982; and in K. Greene, *The Archaeology of the Roman Economy,* London, Batsford, 1986. Placenames are discussed in A.L.F. Rivet and C. Smith, *The Place-names of Roman Britain,* London, Batsford, 1979.

DARK AGES

For the Dark Ages the literature is almost as extensive. The Anglo-Saxon settlements are dealt with in N. Higham, *Rome, Britain and the Anglo-Saxons,* London, Seaby, 1993; C.J. Arnold, *Roman Britain to Saxon England,* London, Croom Helm, 1984; L. Laing and J. Laing, *Celtic Britain and Ireland, c. AD 200–800,* Dublin, Irish Academic Press, 1990; J.E. Cleary, *The Ending of Roman Britain,* London, Batsford, 1989; and C. Hills, 'The Anglo-Saxon Settlement of England' in D. Wilson (ed.), *The Northern World,* London, Thames & Hudson, 1980, pp. 71–94. Other books dealing generally with the Dark Ages and Anglo-Saxon England that will be found useful are D. Wilson, *The Anglo-Saxons,* Harmondsworth, Penguin, 3rd edn, 1981; L. Laing and J. Laing, *Anglo-Saxon England,* London, Routledge & Kegan Paul, 1979; D. Whitelock, *The Beginnings of English Society,* Harmondsworth, Penguin, 1952; L. Alcock, *Arthur's Britain,* Harmondsworth, Allen Lane/Penguin, 1971; and D.M. Wilson (ed.), *The Archaeology of Anglo-Saxon England,* London, Methuen, 1976. Placenames are dealt with in K. Cameron, *English Place-names,* London, Batsford, 3rd edn, 1977. Trade is considered in C.J. Arnold, *The Archaeology of the Early Anglo-Saxon Kingdoms,* London, Routledge, 1988; and art in D.M. Wilson, *Anglo-Saxon Art,* London, Thames & Hudson, 1984. For the history, the standard account remains F.M. Stenton, *Anglo-Saxon England,* Oxford, Oxford University Press, 3rd edn, 1981; or the lavishly illustrated J. Campbell and P. Wormald (eds), *The Anglo-Saxons,* Oxford, Phaidon, 1982. For the language developments in the early part of the period K.H. Jackson, *Language and History in Early Britain,* Cambridge, Cambridge University Press, 1953, despite its date, remains invaluable.

VIKINGS

There are comparatively few books dealing exclusively with the Viking period in Britain. For an introduction to the Vikings in general, readers may find useful E. Roesdahl, *The Vikings*, London, Penguin, 1991; J. Graham-Campbell and D. Kydd, *The Vikings*, London, British Museum, 1980; and J. Graham-Campbell, *The Viking World*, London, Frances Lincoln, 1980. Of the older works, mention perhaps may be made of P.H. Sawyer, *The Age of the Vikings*, London, Arnold, 1971. The best survey for England is perhaps J. Richards, *Viking-Age England*, London, Batsford, 1991, which also deals with late Saxon England; and R. Hall, *Viking Age Archaeology*, Princes Risborough, Shire, 1990. More historical but still valuable is H.R. Loyn, *The Vikings in Britain*, London, Batsford, 1977; although primarily a catalogue, E. Roesdahl (ed.), *The Vikings in England*, London, Anglo-Danish Viking Project, 1981, is also useful. J. Geipel, *The Viking Legacy*, Newton Abbot, David & Charles, 1971, deals primarily with language and institutions. For Scotland there is A. Ritchie, *Viking Scotland*, London, Batsford, 1993; B.E. Crawford, *Scandinavian Scotland*, Leicester, Leicester University Press, 1987; and D. Breeze and A. Ritchie, *Invaders of Scotland*, Edinburgh, HMSO, n.d. but 1991, which as the name suggests is not confined to a discussion of the Vikings. For Jorvik, there is R.A. Hall, *The Viking Dig*, London, Bodley Head, 1984.

MEDIEVAL AND POST-MEDIEVAL

The archaeology in general is covered in H. Clarke, *The Archaeology of Medieval England*, London, Colonnade, 1984, and J.M. Steane, *The Archaeology of Medieval England and Wales*, London, Croom Helm, 1985; the latter is the more comprehensive survey. Also useful and well illustrated is C. Platt, *Medieval England, a Social History and Archaeology from the Conquest to 1600 AD*, London, Routledge & Kegan Paul, 1978. The history is covered in the various volumes of the *Oxford History of England*. Scottish history is dealt with in A.A.M. Duncan, *Scotland, the Making of a Kingdom*, Edinburgh, Oliver & Boyd, 1975; and in W. Croft Dickinson, *Scotland, From the Earliest Times to 1603*, London, Nelson, 1961. A useful survey, which deals in passing with Britain, is J. Evans (ed.), *The Flowering of the Middle Ages*,

London, Thames & Hudson, 1966; the essays by C. Hohler (on court life) and by D. King (on merchants and trade) are particularly useful. The economic history of the period is dealt with in M.W. Thomas (ed.), *A Survey of English Economic History*, London, Blackie, 1957, and E. Lipson, *The Economic History of England, I, The Middle Ages*, London, Black, 1947. The classic study of immigrants to England can be found in W. Cunningham, *Alien Immigrants to England*, (2nd edn, C. Wilson), London, Frank Cass, 1969 (first published 1897). Language is dealt with in M. Serjeantson, *A History of Foreign Words in English*, London, Routledge, 1935. Family names are discussed in P.H. Reaney,*The Origin of English Surnames*, London, Routledge & Kegan Paul, 1967. The literature on the Normans is extensive, but mention may be made of T. Rowley, *The Norman Heritage*, London, Routledge & Kegan Paul, 1983; R.H.C. Davis, *The Normans and their Myth*, London, Thames & Hudson, 1976; R.A. Brown, *The Normans and the Norman Conquest*, London, Constable, 1976; and H.R. Loyn, *The Norman Conquest*, 3rd edn, London, Hutchison, 1982. J. Lindsay, *The Normans and Their World*, London, Granada/Purnell, 1974, offers some stimulating ideas. Castles are dealt with in D.J.C. King, *The Castle in England and Wales*, London, Routledge, 1991, and in R.A. Brown, *English Castles*, 2nd edn, London, Batsford, 1976. The wool trade is discussed in E. Power, *The Wool Trade in English Medieval History*, Oxford, Oxford University Press, 1941. The medieval pottery trade is dealt with in P. Davey and R. Hodges (eds), *Ceramics and Trade*, Sheffield, Sheffield University Press, 1983. Coinage is covered in L. Laing, *Coins and Archaeology*, London, Weidenfeld, 1969; and L.M. Hewlett, *Anglo-Gallic Coins*, London, Baldwin, 1920. The standard account of English coins of all periods is G.C. Brooke, *English Coins*, 3rd edn, London, Methuen, 1950. Art is considered in the three volumes of the Pelican History of Art that are relevant: L. Stone, *Sculpture in Britain: the Middle Ages*, 1955; G. Webb, *Architecture in Britain: The Middle Ages*, 1956; and M. Rickert, *Painting in Britain: The Middle Ages* (rev. edn 1965); all Harmondsworth, Penguin. The Romanesque in general is covered in J. Beckwith, *Early Medieval Art*, London, Thames & Hudson, 1964. A. Martindale, *Gothic Art*, London, Thames & Hudson, 1967, is a useful introduction to that style. Medieval gardens are discussed in J. Harvey, *Mediaeval Gardens*, London, Batsford, 1981; later gardens can be found in

J.D. Hunt and P. Willis, *The Genius of Place, The English Landscape Garden 1620–1820*, London, Elek, 1975. Also useful is C. Taylor, *The Archaeology of Gardens*, Aylesbury, Shire, 1983; and C. Thacker, *The Genius of Gardening*, London, Dent, 1994. For medieval furniture the main reference is P. Eames, *Furniture in England, France and the Netherlands from the Twelfth to the Fifteenth Century*, London, Furniture History Society, 1977. Later furniture is conveniently surveyed in H. Hayward (ed.), *World Furniture*, London, Hamlyn, 1965. Fashion is outlined in J. Laver, *A Concise History of Costume*, London, Thames & Hudson, 1969. A good general introduction to pottery in England can be found in W.B. Honey, *English Pottery and Porcelain*, London, A. & C. Black, 6th edn, rev. R.J. Charleston, 1969.

Index